MATHEMATICS SUCCESS AND FAILURE AMONG AFRICAN-AMERICAN YOUTH

The Roles of Sociohistorical Context, Community Forces, School Influence, and Individual Agency

STUDIES IN MATHEMATICAL THINKING
AND LEARNING

Alan H. Schoenfeld, Series Editor

MATHEMATICS SUCCESS AND FAILURE AMONG AFRICAN-AMERICAN YOUTH

The Roles of Sociohistorical Context, Community Forces, School Influence, and Individual Agency

Danny Bernard Martin
Contra Costa College

LAWRENCE ERLBAUM ASSOCIATES, PUBLISHERS
2000   Mahwah, New Jersey   London

The final camera copy for this work was prepared by the author, and therefore the publisher takes no responsibility for consistency or correctness of typographical style. However, this arrangement helps to make publication of this kind of scholarship possible.

A DI-4412

Lawrence Erlbaum Associates, Inc., Publishers
10 Industrial Avenue
Mahwah, New Jersey 07430

Cover design by Kathryn Houghtaling Lacey

Library of Congress Cataloging-in-Publication Data

Maartin, Danny Bernard.
    Mathematics success and failure among African-American youth : the roles of sociohistorical context, community forces, school influence, and individual agency / Danny Bernard Martin.
        p.   cm. -- (Studies in mathematical thinking and learning)
    Includes bibliographical references and index.
    ISBN 0-8058-3042-1 (cloth : alk. paper)
    1. Mathematics--Study and teaching--United States. 2. Afro
-American students--Education.   I. Title.   II. Series.
QA13.M145   1999
510'.71'0973--dc21   99-34928
                                                                          CIP

Books published by Lawrence Erlbaum Associates are printed on acid-free paper, and their bindings are chosen for strength and durability.

Printed in the United States of America
10   9   8   7   6   5   4   3   2   1

Contents

Preface

No matter how mathematics achievement and persistence are measured, African-Americans lag behind their peers. Instances of success can be found, but disproportionately poor results remain the norm despite promises of change found in mathematics education reforms and significant advances in mathematics education research.

This book, which is both a personal and professional project, is the result of my efforts to understand mathematics success and failure among African-American youth. In it I address learning, teaching, classroom interactions, and curricula. These are typical areas of concern among mathematics education researchers. But, in my view, the mathematics education of African-Americans does not unfold solely in schools that are hermetically sealed from other influences, past and present. This book is also about history and context. It is about history because the mathematical experiences of the African-American parents and community members profiled in this book cannot be discussed apart from their larger socioeconomic and educational experiences or the treatment they have received over the course of their lives as a result of their African-American status.

This book is about context because the mathematical experiences of African-American parents and students are subject to a variety of interrelated contextual influences. These include the sociohistorical, community, family, school, and intrapersonal forces that have an impact on their academic and mathematical development at both individual and collective levels.

Based on data I collected in two cities, I argue that there are explanatory streams for mathematics success and failure among African-American youth that span sociohistorical, community, family, school, and intrapersonal contexts. My analysis suggests that because prior studies have failed to link contextual forces in sufficiently meaningful or complex ways, these studies can be characterized by both theoretical and methodological limitations—limitations that have hindered the ability of mathematics educators to reverse the negative achievement and persistence trends that continue to affect these students.

I open this book by describing how my experiences as a student and teacher of mathematics led me to investigate mathematics success and failure among African-American youth. My initial research design had some of the same limitations as prior studies. I describe how I altered my study to include history and context.

Chapter 1 sets the stage by reviewing and critiquing existing perspectives of mathematics achievement and persistence among African-Americans. I then present the capstone of my research: a multilevel framework that I believe allows one to trace out the explanatory streams just described and to identify mechanisms that produce both mathematics success and failure among African-Americans.

This context-based framework brings together theory and methods from sociocultural perspectives on schooling and cognitive perspectives on mathematics learning. A cultural perspective was useful because it allowed me to better understand why mathematics learning and knowledge assumed the meanings they did among the participants by considering those relevant, mathematics-related experiences that influenced these meanings. These experiences were characterized as an important component of the participants' *mathematics socializations.*

From a cognitive perspective, these socially and culturally constructed meanings for mathematics are thought of as acting at a psychological level. They are discussed in the context of what I call *mathematics identity*—one's beliefs about his or her mathematics abilities, one's beliefs about the instrumental importance of mathematics, one's beliefs about opportunities and constraints that exist to participate in mathematics, and one's motivation to obtain mathematics knowledge.

Chapter 2 discusses *cultural and community beliefs about mathematics.* I describe aspects of the mathematical experiences of four African-American parents and community members. These 4 were selected from a larger pool of 10, all of whom participated in extended interviews. These four narratives will highlight a particular collection of socioeconomic and educational experiences that dramatically affected the participants' mathematics identities and their expectations and goals for themselves and for their children. Readers will see that even in such a small sample, African-American adults have insightful and compelling stories to tell about their mathematical experiences. Moreover, embedded within each of these stories are clues to the achievement and persistence problems that continue to affect large numbers of African-American students.

Chapter 3 discusses various school-level forces at Hillside that contributed to students' in-school mathematics socializations. These forces included the role of teachers as agents of mathematics socialization; the role of peers in mathematics socialization; and the ways in which classroom and curricular practices served as contexts that promoted positive or negative mathematics socialization and identity. My interviews with and observations of teachers and students at Hillside revealed that there was a strong norm of underachievement among most of the students. This norm negatively influenced many students' in-class behaviors and also contributed to their beliefs about and resistance to many of the reform-oriented practices stressed in the Algebra Project curriculum. Chapter 3 details the effects of this resistance on mathematics learning and teaching at Hillside.

At its core, this book is concerned with the psychological, academic, and mathematical development of African-American adolescents, viewed in the context of the various forces that come to bear on their development. Although I was troubled by the large number of students who experienced low motivation and underachievement at Hillside, I also wanted to know why and how some students managed to achieve academic and mathematics success. Many studies of mathematics achievement and persistence among African-American students appear to be based on perspectives that imply that these students are passive recipients of differential treatment from their teachers, are unable to resist and negotiate the norms of the peer cultures in their schools and the curricular practices found in their classrooms, and are unable to succeed because of the circumstances that define their lives outside of school. But I believe there is much more to be said about the agency and resiliency of African-American students as well as about the relationships between their mathematics identities and other identities they construct. Chapter 4 focuses on academically and mathematically successful students at Hillside. It presents 7 case studies—selected from a pool of 35—and discusses the factors that influenced these students' success in light of the discussions in chapters 2 and 3.

Chapter 5, the final chapter of this book, ties together the analyses presented in chapters 2, 3, and 4. My discussion also returns to the context-based framework that I introduce in chapter 1 and highlights important relationships between the themes outlined in that framework. I conclude the chapter and book by discussing the implications of this work.

Using an ethnographic approach and working within contexts of sociohistorical, community, school, curricular, and intrapersonal forces, this book adds complexity to discussions of mathematics learning, achievement, and persistence among African-Americans. It also contributes to a needed reconceptualization (Secada, 1992, 1995) of these issues by showing that there are strong relationships between mathematics success and failure among African-Americans and their mathematics socializations within and across the contexts already mentioned. In my view, studies that focus on mathematics content and curriculum in isolation from the contextual forces that affect the lives of students, parents, and teachers will do little to address differential student learning, achievement, and persistence issues in mathematics. The data and analyses presented in this book help to fill the gap between knowledge gained from studies of mathematics content and knowledge gained from studies of context and culture.

I do not claim that the discussion presented here generalizes to all African-Americans or that I have addressed all the important theoretical and methodological issues affecting mathematics achievement and persistence among them. No book can. What I have done in this book is to take a relatively small piece of the education pie for African-Americans—mathematics achievement and persistence—and attempted to examine these issues in light of ongoing achievement and persistence problems and the lack of compelling explanations for them. I am well aware that much of the explanation for problematic educational outcomes among African-Americans lies in analyses of public policy, racial stratification, poverty, and many other issues (e.g., Comer, 1980; Haynes & Comer, 1990; Wilson, 1987, 1996). Although my theoretical framework is limited in the sense that it does not—and cannot—span all of these contextual forces, the results that I do present are, nevertheless, important.

The significance of this book is that it adds to our understanding of how mathematics success and failure among African-Americans are affected by contextual forces that extend beyond the school setting. I explain, in detail, how African-Americans' experiences with these forces characterize their mathematics socializations and shape their mathematics identities. By discussing how African American students and parents invoke their agency in response to these forces, I also show how these contextual forces are not as deterministic as some research suggests. It is precisely these kinds of context-agency relationships and explanations of mathematics success and failure that are absent in prior studies. The more we know about these relationships, the more effective we can be in developing strategies that help African-Americans succeed in mathematics.

This book will prove to be useful and informative to many groups—mathematics education researchers, mathematicians, education researchers interested in the social context of learning and teaching, teachers, teacher education students, policy makers, parents, community advocates, and students. This book will also be of interest to readers concerned with multicultural education, cross-cultural studies of mathematics learning, sociology of education, Black Studies, and issues of underrepresentation in science and mathematics. Because it includes history and context, the theoretical framework may be of use in its own right in analyzing the educational situations of other groups for whom history and context play important roles, such as the Native Americans in the United States, the Aboriginals in Australia, and the Maori in New Zealand.

ACKNOWLEDGMENTS

Although this book bears my name as the sole author, it has benefitted greatly from the assistance that I received from colleagues and friends. For those whom I mention in the following paragraphs, I extend a special thanks. For those who are not mentioned but to whom I am equally indebted, your help and timely advice were greatly appreciated.

First, I express my deepest and most sincere gratitude to Alan H. Schoenfeld. Professor Schoenfeld, who served as my dissertation chair at the University of California, Berkeley, has continued to be an intellectual inspiration. His penetrating insight into complex issues as well as his ability to offer subtle suggestions have greatly affected my research and the writing of this book. His willingness to read, discuss, and comment on my work without hesitation often went beyond the call of duty. I thank him for being a positive and scholarly role model and mentor. I am honored to have shared and improved my ideas with such a talented thinker, researcher, and writer.

Second, I express deep gratitude to John U. Ogbu, who served as my dissertation co-chair. It was Professor Ogbu who first led me to consider the importance of sociohistorical and community forces and issues of cultural meaning and who suggested that I think about their relevance to my own work. Professor Ogbu's insightful and important works have served as constant sources of inspiration and have caused me to reorganize my thinking about a very complex set of issues.

I owe special thanks to Emily van Zee and Pedro Noguera, both of whom served on my dissertation committee. Professor van Zee's suggestion that I focus on successful students has greatly benefited this work. Professor Noguera is an eloquent scholar on school-level issues and school-community relations. I learned a great deal from his suggestions and recommendations.

As a beginning graduate student, I was enlighted by the teaching of Mary Elizabeth Brenner. Professor Brenner's wealth of knowledge eased my transition from mathematics to mathematics education. She was the first person to encourage me to pursue the issues in this book rigorously. Her encouragement made me feel that I would be able to contribute toward the solution of a difficult problem.

I also thank the members of the Functions research group at the University of California, Berkeley, for their efforts to understand my ideas and for offering me valuable feedback and advice on the research in this book. I especially thank my two dear friends Ming Ming Chiu and Juila Aguirre.

As I began to prepare this book for publication, Cathy Kessel came to my aid and agreed to review and edit hundreds of pages of my manuscript. Her keen eye, attention to detail, and many helpful suggestions have improved this book tremendously.

I thank the University of California, Berkeley, for providing me with generous support while a graduate student in mathematics and later in mathematics education. A National Academy of Education postdoctoral fellowship, administered the Spencer Foundation, supported the revision of my dissertation into this book and is allowing me to continue studying the issues raised in my doctoral research.

I also thank my wife, Rachelle, who grew to undertand how important this work is to me.

Finally, to the students and teachers at Hillside Junior High and the parents and community members who allowed me to tell their stories in this book, I dedicate this book to you.

Danny Bernard Martin

Introduction

"Danny, I just wanted to let you to know that I've recommended you for the accelerated math class when you begin seventh grade next year."

Those words were spoken to me by my sixth-grade teacher in the spring of 1977. As I look back on that experience, more than 20 years later, I realize that I had no way of fully recognizing the significance of what my teacher was saying. Nor did I know that I was being put on a path in life where I would encounter few other African-Americans and where trying to understand the difficult and complex issues associated with mathematics learning, achievement, and persistence among African-Americans would become my life's work. Beginning that next year, my friends and I simply went to different math classes. The reality of African-American underrepresentation in mathematics would become even more apparent in high school, where I was one of just three Black students enrolled in the accelerated math courses. This pattern continued through my years as an undergraduate student in mathematics and physics and as a graduate student in both mathematics and mathematics education. The more advanced the course, the smaller the proportion of African-American students.

For the last 10 years, I have taught mathematics to middle school, high school, community college, and university students. At the community college where I now teach, I am the only full-time, African-American faculty member in the department of mathematics and only the third in the school's history. This school, it should be noted, is located in a city with a large African-American population, a fact that is also reflected in the composition of the school's student body. Since being hired by this school, I have taught nearly every mathematics course offered. Along the way, I have noticed the same pattern that I first saw twenty years ago: many African-American students are enrolled in remedial or lower-level mathematics courses and few go on to take Precalculus, Calculus, or higher-level courses.

I have not stood by idly and done nothing to try and reverse this pattern. During the last 10 years, I have participated in a number of

1

mathematics education projects whose goals were to attract African-American students to mathematics and to help them succeed at it. Despite the success achieved by some of these programs, I am well aware that a disproportionate number of these students still do not reach their potential in mathematics or persist in studying it.

As a teacher and researcher, I continue to struggle with the questions of why African-Americans remain underrepresented in mathematics and why large numbers of Black students achieve below their potential. Colleagues with whom I have worked over the years have frequently asked me to explain why more African-American students do not enroll in higher level math courses at the college and high school levels, why these students begin disappearing from the mathematics pipeline as early as elementary school, and why promises of changes from both research and reform movements have had little effect on reversing these trends. For a long time, my answers to these questions were mostly of an improvised nature—answers constructed to deal with the situations at hand.

It was not until I began to pursue these issues rigorously that I became fully aware of their complexity and began looking for compelling explanations. Such explanations would have to indicate why problematic mathematics achievement and persistence outcomes are not confined to a few students but have continued to affect a large proportion of African-American students regardless of their socioeconomic status, family background, grade level, or type of school attended.

In the Fall of 1993, I was in the early stages of my dissertation research. I had recently begun ethnographic observations in a school that I will call Hillside Junior High School, a predominantly African-American school in Oakland, California. I was attracted to Hillside because the school was in the process of implementing the Algebra Project Transition Curriculum, an experience-based curriculum that was being used in a number of middle school sites around the country—middle schools with large numbers of African-American students (Moses, Kamii, Swap, & Howard, 1989; Silva & Moses, 1990). This curriculum, developed by civil rights activist Robert Moses, was designed to help Black students mathematize their experiences in real-world contexts using a highly successful five-step learning process. Many of the practices stressed in this curriculum—experiential learning, mathematical communication, cooperative learning, emphasis on multiple representations, and problem solving—are consistent with those called for in the current mathematics education reform movement.

Middle school is an important period in students' mathematical education. It is where important decisions are made about which students go to algebra and, perhaps, college-track mathematics. I knew that the Algebra Project curriculum was intended to help African-American students with the transition from arithmetic to formal algebra, thereby providing them with access to courses in this college track and the skills needed to succeed in them. Hillside seemed an ideal place to study African-American students' construction of their mathematical knowledge, the mathematical culture and success that the Algebra Project had produced elsewhere, as well as the "algebra for all" philosophy embedded in the curriculum.

The initial formulation of my research plan was straightforward. Consistent with most mainstream research in mathematics education, I thought that a strict focus on mathematical content, curriculum, and problem-solving behaviors would be the best way to understand mathematics achievement and persistence issues among African-American students. I did not want to make my task any more difficult by addressing social and cultural factors because I believed it would only distract me from my study of the day to day activities in classrooms and the doing of mathematics.

After a few weeks at Hillside, however, I saw that things were not going as planned. Most troubling was the large number of students who experienced low motivation and low achievement and who engaged in behaviors that had an adverse affect on the teaching and learning of mathematics. For many students, there were issues with their beliefs about what counted as mathematics and their beliefs about the importance of mathematics in relation to other aspects of their daily lives. I also observed many students who struggled with the social and mathematical demands placed on them by the new practices stressed in their classrooms. I often heard comments like "I hate math." and "Math is boring." Rather than rush to judgment, I wanted to better understand what I was observing.

In my search for explanations, I first turned to the relatively small literature that already existed on African-American students and mathematics. Although those studies were informative and presented extensive data on the scope of underachievement and limited persistence among African-Americans, they were, for the most part, confined to four categories of explanation: (1) analyses of achievement tests and claims about student ability, (2) studies of tracking and differential treatment, (3) studies of student attitudes and course taking patterns, and (4) studies of family background and socioeconomic status. My questions about students and teachers at Hillside were either not addressed by studies in these areas or were addressed in overly simple ways. I had a difficult time accepting the fact that the complexity that was typically found elsewhere in discussions of student learning, teaching, curriculum development and change, and assessment was absent in these studies. Explanations of student learning, for example, were often more robust than references to student ability. This higher standard of explanation did not carry over into many of the studies of mathematics achievement and persistence among African-American students.

The dispositions and behaviors that I observed among students at Hillside were not due to student ability, content difficulty or biased curriculum. Most students, when given support and direction, could exhibit the kind of mathematical understanding that the teachers expected. Also, the students were working with a curriculum that was specifically designed to take advantage of their real-world experiences and to make mathematics more meaningful to them.

These students' behaviors were not a matter of teacher attitudes. My observations of and interactions with the teachers at Hillside suggested that they were extremely committed to their students. They worked very hard to establish and achieve student-centered and content-centered goals. The math teachers, all of whom were African or African-American, often spoke about their students in ways that suggested that their concerns were not based on mere academic grounds but represented their wishes for the betterment of the African-American community. In that regard, the teachers were willing to be openly critical of both students and parents.

Finally, the achievement and motivational problems among the students were not determined, in any straightforward way, by students' family and socioeconomic backgrounds. School-district data showed that in the 1993–1994 school year Hillside had the fourth highest socioeconomic ranking among Oakland's 16 middle schools, ranking only behind three schools that served mostly middle-class and more affluent students. Moreover, some Hillside students from middle-class backgrounds did poorly while some from disadvantaged backgrounds did well.

Student ability, tracking, biased curricula and pedagogy, and family background are critically important considerations in mathematics learning, achievement, and persistence among African-American students but, in my view, it is clear that they do not fully explain the problem.

My search for explanations also led me to examine studies in mainstream mathematics education research. Here, I mean studies of mathematics content, learning, and teaching. I found that despite significant advances in research—advances which have lead to increased understandings of how students learn, how teachers teach, and improved methods of assessing teachers and students—very little of this research addressed what I consider to be one of the most troubling issues in mathematics education: differential student learning, achievement, and persistence along ethnic and racial lines.

It became apparent that I was not going to be able to explain what was I observing at Hillside in ways that I had anticipated. Because the behaviors and dispositions that I observed among students could not have been formed in the few weeks since the beginning of the school year, I began to look for deeper connections between school-level factors and the sociohistorical and community contexts in which schools like Hillside are embedded. My inclination to do so was bolstered by the comments and actions of teachers and students, as well as by suggestions made by members of my dissertation committee. Educational anthropologist John Ogbu and mathematics educator Alan Schoenfeld suggested that I examine aspects of historical and community forces and try to connect these issues to mathematics achievement and persistence.

I turned to various literatures outside of mathematics education, including those in educational anthropology, urban education, and sociology of education, where I was intrigued by discussions of culture, ethnicity, stratification, opportunity structure, and African-American status. Although informative, many of the studies in these areas made it seem that ethnicity, culture, class, and opportunity structure were deterministic—ignoring the human agency and individual motivation that can result in spite of these larger forces (Bandura, 1982, 1986). I witnessed such agency on a daily basis among students and teachers at Hillside. This agency was an especially important component of student's learning.

A second criticism that I had was that I found few studies that narrowed their focus to issues of mathematics learning and teaching in ways that were meaningful to me as a mathematics educator. Yet, I knew these ideas could be made more meaningful. In my teaching experiences with African-American adults, I often became a sounding board for their individual and collective stories. These stories linked cultural, community, societal, and structural forces not just to their own mathematical experiences but to those of their children.

I reformulated my earlier questions about mathematics culture at Hillside, adding to them questions about the natures of larger contextual forces and their effects on African-American students' mathematical development. This meant that I had to examine not only the mathematics experiences of the students and teachers at Hillside but also the mathematics-related experiences of African-American parents and community members. I found myself asking questions such as: What were the nature of these experiences? What where their enduring effects? Could there be intergenerational dialogues, either implicit or explicit, that were taking place about the importance of mathematics knowledge? To what degree did parents become advocates for their children in mathematics? What were the various academic trajectories of students as a result of these influences? In many ways, this was a reversal of my earlier stance on social and cultural considerations. To better understand what was happening inside the school, I had to go outside of it.

A very brief example of what I found—one that highlights the more troubling aspects of African American parents' prior mathematical experiences—comes from an interview that I conducted with a 55-year-old African-American father whom I call Harold. Early in the interview, I asked Harold to think back to his formative years and tell me what he remembered. His comments focused a great deal on his beliefs about racism and the differential treatment that he experienced. When I asked him if and how his experiences affected his educational motivation and commitment, he responded:

> Yes, those things did affect my schooling. . . . Because I saw that I was going to eventually be a laborer someplace, you know. I could see those jobs out there. I could see what aptitude and what kind of personality was required to do what was made available to me. But I didn't pursue any more sophisticated means of employment simply because I wasn't encouraged that the opportunity was there. So, I only indulged myself in my studies to the degree that I was satisfied that I could do math up to multiplication and division of fractions and decimals, and that was good enough for me for what I was going to do. I wasn't going to be doing any math.

The effect of Harold's experiences was not limited to his mathematics education. Later in the interview, their potentially devastating effects on the education of his teenage son became clear:

> My expectations of [my son]? I really don't have no expectations. I have some hopes. My expectation is that he will graduate from high school. If he doesn't, it's no big deal. . . . My expectation for him is to probably be no worse than I was. Just to pass. . . . I think he's had as much [education] as he needs. Elementary school is enough

schooling to get you along in society. . . . He's learned all the basic
things there is like how to go out and get a general laborer's job.

In subsequent chapters, I discuss why sociohistorical and community forces, as part of a multilevel framework, help to explain why mathematics learning and teaching unfolded in the ways they did at Hillside. A major goal of this book is to describe the natures of these forces, their relation to school forces, and African-American students', parents, and community members' responses to these forces.

In presenting my data, I have made a deliberate decision to utilize as much of the participants' own words as possible. In doing so, the themes in my framework do not simply represent theoretical notions but are grounded in the real-life experiences of African-American adolescents, adults, and their teachers. My rationale is similar to that adopted by Weis and Fine (1996) in a recent study of the views of poor and working class White and African-American men. In that study they used the term "data heavy" to describe their tendency to present extended transcript excerpts from these men's interviews. The authors justified their presentation of these "biographies of race" in the following way:

> We appreciate hearing the voices of those who are generally not heard. In this case...the data are so compelling that we urge the reader to work through the interviewee's points. Rarely are [these voices] heard as more and more policies are made in their name. . . . While we do understand that this is our *discursive* product, in the sense that we did the interviews, coded the data and wrote the article, we also believe in the integrity of the men's voices and wish them, in so far as possible, to be heard on their own terms. . . . Additionally, we made a decision to include lengthy segments of these men's narratives so that they could be heard speaking in *their* context and in their own voice rather than our simply extracting snippets of their words to fit our conceptual frame. (p. 497)

Studies of mathematics achievement and persistence among African-Americans have often relied on the analysis and presentation of aggregated test-taking data, with little attention or voice given to the individuals in these studies. It is my sincere hope that the data, theoretical framework, and results presented here provide such a voice and contribute to a greater understanding of the mathematics education of African-American students, and ultimately, to increased success in mathematics for all students.

1

Mathematics Learning, Achievement, and Persistence Among African-Americans:

Toward a Context-Based Perspective

Why is it that African-Americans remain underrepresented and continue to perform below their potential in mathematics?

Given the history of African-Americans in the United States, a big-picture explanation might suggest that these outcomes are the legacies of mathematical experiences characterized by differential treatment and denied opportunity in socioeconomic and educational contexts. Woodson (1933/1990), an African-American historian and educator, discussed this historical-legacy point of view as early as 1933:

> Negroes, then learned from their oppressors to say to their children that there were certain spheres into which they should not go because they would have no chance therein for development. In a number of places young men and women were discouraged or frightened away from certain professions by the poor showing made by those trying to function in them. . . . In the same way, the Negro was once discouraged and dissuaded from taking up designing, drafting, architecture, engineering and chemistry. (pp. 50–51)

Contemporary scholars (e.g., Jones, 1993; Ladson-Billings, 1994, 1995; Oakes, 1990a, 1990b; Tate, 1994, 1995) also raised this issue in discussions of mathematics achievement and persistence among African-Americans. A counterargument to claims by Woodson and others, and one that I believe is far too simple, would suggest that societal changes have led to increased economic and educational opportunities for everyone, including African-Americans, in all aspects of life. This argument continues by suggesting that because members of other cultural groups have managed to excel in areas like

8

mathematics, problematic outcomes in mathematics achievement and persistence among African-Americans must, in part, reflect lack of ability and effort or some other pathology.

A thorough search of the literature in mathematics education reveals that there exist few studies or theoretical perspectives that account for the schism between these explanations. Why is it, for example, that despite increased demand for those who possess mathematics-related skills and knowledge, significant advances in educational theory, and calls for higher educational standards, African-Americans continue to experience their mathematics educations in ways that place them at or near the bottom of all measures of achievement and persistence?

Several studies have examined mathematics achievement and persistence among African-Americans from a variety of other perspectives. (e.g., Anick, Carpenter, & Smith, 1981; Betz, 1991; Carey, Fennema, Carpenter, & Franke, 1995; Dossey, Mullis, Lindquist, & Chambers, 1988; Johnson, 1989; Matthews, 1984; Matthews, Carpenter, Lindquist, & Silver, 1984; Moses, 1994; Oakes, 1990a, 1990b; Orr, 1987; Post, Stewart, & Smith, 1991; Secada, 1992, 1995; Secada, Ogbu, Peterson, Stiff, & Tonemah, 1994; Silver, Smith, & Nelson, 1995; Stanic, 1991; Stanic & Hart, 1995; Tate, 1994, 1995; Treisman, 1985). These studies have raised many important and provocative questions about the potential causes of underachievement and limited persistence in mathematics among Black students.

For example, some researchers have sought to determine if there are cultural and linguistic barriers that hinder African-American students' performance in mathematics. This is evidenced by studies that have focused on learning styles and the use of Black English (e.g., Orr, 1987). Other studies have raised questions about students' family and socioeconomic backgrounds, suggesting that there are important relations between parent education levels and student achievement.

Examining relations between societal forces and schooling, some researchers have focused on the devastating effects of racism and discrimination, asking whether structural and institutional forces have served as barriers that block African-Americans' access to lucrative technical areas that are dependent on the study of mathematics (Wilson, 1987, 1996). These considerations have caused some mathematics educators to conceptualize mathematics persistence and achievement issues in civil rights terms (Moses, 1994).

In addition to asking questions about societal and cultural factors, questions have also been raised about African-American students' treatment in schools and their interactions with in-school practices. Do African-American students have access to the best teachers and high-quality instructional and learning materials? Do teachers develop low expectations for African-American students, treat them unfairly, and track them out of mathematics (e.g., Oakes, 1985, 1990a, 1990b)?

A growing literature has been devoted to discussing multi-culturalism and culturally compatible pedagogy in mathematics (e.g., Frankenstein, 1995; Ladson-Billings, 1993, 1994). In these studies, researchers have asked whether the curriculum and pedagogical styles currently used in schools are compatible with the academic needs and learning styles of African-American students. This focus highlights the fact that if curricula and pedagogy do not connect mathematics to the everyday lives of students in sufficiently meaningful ways, students may disengage from activities that they do not see as important or relevant.

When we systematically examine each of these perspectives on African-American achievement and persistence in mathematics, what is it that we do and do not learn?

STUDENT ABILITY

Results from large-scale tests of mathematics achievement such as the National Assessment of Educational Progress (NAEP) have been equally enlightening and troubling. These results show that, as a group, Black students typically score below their peers in all content areas of mathematics. Moreover, these achievement differences grow as the topic areas increase in complexity (Anick et al., 1981; Dossey et al., 1988; Johnson, 1984, 1989; Jones, Burton, & Davenport, 1984). Although there have been some achievement gains among African-American students since the mid-1980s, these improvements have occurred mostly on those sections of tests related to basic skills.

Because of the need to understand the status and progress of African-American student achievement in mathematics, the attention and weight given to test scores is, in many ways, warranted and well deserved. These tests have helped point out that there continue to be differences in the amount of mathematics learned among different student groups. On the other hand, these studies provide no evidence that Black students differ from their peers in their capacity to learn mathematics.

Moreover, despite an abundance of literature that describes failure among Black students, very little research explains why some of these students succeed in mathematics and why they do so at levels comparable to their peers in other ethnic groups (e.g., Treisman, 1985). Why might this be true? Are there contextual or motivational variables present among these students that achievement tests alone cannot measure? Few researchers have analyzed within-group differences in achievement among African-American students or the factors that contribute to similar mathematics achievement levels across different student groups.

This book addresses within-group achievement and motivational differences among African-American students by examining factors that contribute to both success and failure in mathematics.

ATTITUDE AND ACHIEVEMENT: AN INTERESTING PARADOX

Research suggesting differences in cognitive ability in mathematics has provided little convincing evidence that such differences exist (Ginsburg & Russell, 1981). In many cases, these studies have been shown to rest on racially biased assumptions and appeals to cultural-deficit theories (e.g., Herrnstein & Murray, 1994). There is growing evidence, however, that research on affective variables may be effective in showing that students from different minority groups respond differently to schooling practices and that these different responses can affect academic achievement (e.g., Carr, 1996; Eccles, Lord, & Midgeley, 1991; Graham, 1994; Hart & Allexsaht-Snider, 1996; Meece, 1991; McLeod, 1992; Mickelson, 1990; Ogbu, 1988, 1990, 1992a, 1992b, 1993; Reyes, 1984; Samimy, Liu, & Matsuta, 1994).

This is an important point because studies of mathematics learning that take history into account have shown that the motivation and tendency to participate and perform in areas like mathematics often has a basis that extends beyond the school context to include sociohistorical and socioeconomic factors (e.g., Bishop, 1988; Gay & Cole, 1967; Nunes, 1992; Saxe, 1992). Data from cross-cultural studies confirm that there are, indeed, differences in the ways that parents and students from different cultural groups regard the importance of mathematics (Stevenson & Stigler, 1992). In particular, researchers have pointed out that as a result of discrimination, racism, and the evolution of certain societal roles and occupational patterns, members of particular groups often develop and refine skills that are appropriate and useful in certain cultural niches but are less likely, less motivated, or not allowed to develop skills needed in other areas. Over time, both structural and cultural forces make it more likely that these groups' members remain in those roles and therefore more difficult for them to focus their efforts and abilities elsewhere (Bowles & Gintis, 1976; Willis, 1977).

One interesting case is the participation in mathematics and science-based fields by many Asian-American groups. Tsang (1988), for example, indicated that sociohistorical forces, in addition to ability and effort, may account for the fact that Asian-American groups are overrepresented in these areas. Historically speaking, members of these groups were often denied opportunities and faced discrimination in others areas of U.S. society but, for a number of reasons, were allowed to work in mathematics and science-based areas.

In mathematics education, most of what is known about the mathematical beliefs and attitudes of African-Americans is based on large-scale survey data. At the student level, for example, NAEP and other data show that African-American children consistently express the most positive attitudes toward mathematics among all student groups. Other studies show that many African-American students identify mathematics as one of their favorite and most important subjects despite having very weak conceptions about its utility (e.g., Matthews, 1984; Stanic & Hart, 1995).

Despite these promising results, interpreting the data on mathematical beliefs among Black students has proven to be difficult. Although they express the most positive attitudes about mathematics, African-American students continue to experience very low achievement rates. This inconsistency remains unexplained by conventional perspectives and highlights the fact that, beyond knowing how they might define mathematics as a school subject, we know very little about their beliefs concerning its instrumental importance and value in broader, nonschool contexts. More generally, we know very little about the ways African-Americans situate and give meaning to mathematics knowledge in the context of their everyday life experiences, their socioeconomic and educational goals, and their beliefs about their ability or inability to reap rewards based on mathematics knowledge.

There is a clear need to expand the knowledge base of mathematical beliefs among African-Americans beyond data that has been collected using survey methods. This was accomplished using individual and small-group ethnographic interviews (Eisenhart, 1988). These methods, if used more frequently, would inform us more directly about the mathematical experiences of African-Americans, including their beliefs about constraints and opportunities in mathematical contexts, the ways in which they define the value of mathematics knowledge, their motivations to learn or do mathematics, and the significant aspects of their experiences that cause them to value mathematics in the ways that they do. Using these methods would also represent an effective way to investigate claims by those who advocate a more critical perspective within mathematics education—characterizing mathematics as a filter for access to privilege (e.g., Atweh, Bleicher, & Cooper, 1995; Moses, 1994; Stanic, 1991; Tate, 1995). Whether African-Americans, who have been the victims of denied privilege, view mathematics in this manner, associate it with opportunistic advantage, and respond in ways that affect their performance and persistence are interesting empirical questions.

This book offers viable hypotheses as to how these questions may be answered. The analysis suggests that African-American parents and community members do express beliefs consistent with the dominant societal folk theories of mathematics learning. But their life experiences are such that they also express beliefs that reflect perceptions of their limited opportunity to participate in mathematical contexts as a result of differential treatment based on their African-American status.

In addition, interviews with African-American students showed that, although they recognized mathematics as an important school subject, there were differences in the ways in which successful and unsuccessful students extended these meanings and invoked their individual agency to act on these meanings. Successful students were more likely to recognize the instrumental importance of mathematics, express high levels of confidence in their abilities, and suggest that mathematics was a necessary ingredient to achieving their goals in life. This was an encouraging finding because it indicates that some students can be encouraged to invest in mathematics in light of or despite the experiences of the adults who surround them. Unsuccessful students also recognized the importance of mathematics but, unfortunately, did not demonstrate the same kind of attitudinal and behavioral investment made by their more successful peers. In fact, many unsuccessful students appeared to have been more heavily influenced by the negative beliefs about school and mathematics that were found in their peer groups.

BLACK AND HISPANIC KIDS OVER HERE
WHITE AND ASIAN KIDS OVER THERE

In addition to studies investigating group test-taking trends and attitude differences, other studies have focused on the effects of school-level practices on mathematics achievement, persistence, and opportunity to learn. For example, studies have documented that African-American students are disproportionately tracked out of mainstream mathematics and science curricula into remedial and vocational mathematics. This tracking has been shown to be fixed, long-term, and to cover all grade levels (Oakes, 1985, 1990b).

Although tracking as an institutional mechanism leading to differential learning opportunities for African-American students has been well documented, findings have not been as clear when the focus of analysis has been narrowed to individual teachers. This is, in part, because concepts such as *teacher attitude* have remained largely underdefined (Hart, 1989). Researchers in mathematics education are only now beginning to present characterizations of the beliefs and practices that are detailed enough to give meaning to teachers' actions, especially their interactions with African-American students (e.g., Ladson-Billings, 1994; Stanic & Hart, 1995). For example, recent studies have focused on the content and curricular demands placed on teachers as well as their preparation and competency (e.g., Brown & Borko, 1992; Fennema & Franke, 1992; Noddings, 1992; Thompson, 1985, 1992). Other studies have focused on teachers' educational and life histories, their beliefs about ideal ways of knowing and doing, their beliefs about and expectations for their students, and their beliefs about their students' parents and communities. These latter studies, many of which have been conducted outside of mathematics education, have attempted to focus on both subject-matter knowledge and diversity issues (e.g., Delpit, 1988; King, 1991; Shulman & Mesa-Bains, 1990; Smith, 1995; Winfield, 1986).

In short, what we are learning from these studies of teachers is that "a variety of factors interact with teacher conceptions in affecting their classroom behavior" (Thompson, 1985, p. 283). This implies that rather than reflecting biases against students based on their ethnic and language backgrounds, teachers' interactions with students are affected by a number of demands on their teaching. They respond to these demands by demonstrating a variety of complex behaviors and sending a variety of mixed messages about mathematics to their students. It is my contention that these beliefs and behaviors and the messages they send form an integral part of the mathematics socialization process that African-American students undergo in school and classroom contexts.

Finally, it also has been also claimed that differential treatment of African-American students is reflected at a curricular level. Such claims are based on the assumption that because curricular materials are based on White, middle-class standards of knowledge, they are biased against students from certain ethnic and language backgrounds. In response to these concerns, some researchers have attempted to design and document pedagogical and curricular practices that are particularly effective with African-American students (e.g., Carey et al., 1995; Ladson-Billings, 1994, 1995; Moses et al., 1989; Silver et al., 1995). Several researchers have suggested efforts such as multicultural curricula, culturally relevant pedagogy, and experientially based curricula as remedies for differential treatment and cultural discontinuities. These efforts are grounded in the idea that by taking advantage of students' cultural knowledge and incorporating cultural elements and images into their classroom experiences, students are more likely to consider these activities as relevant to their lives. Until recently, few published studies focused on the effects of these efforts on student achievement and persistence in mathematics (e.g., Ladson-Billings, 1993, 1994; Moses et al., 1989). These studies show that teachers who engage in culturally relevant pedagogy can be very effective in assisting African-American students to negotiate the classroom and curricular practices they encounter. However, the weight given by these researchers to pedagogical and curricular change alone as remedies for African-American student underperformance is problematic because many Black students achieve at high levels even in schools and classrooms where these positive practices are not found. Moreover, many of the most successful mathematics students, especially some Asian American students, come from non-White, poor, limited-English backgrounds and they, too, often achieve at the highest levels in spite of the curriculum and classroom practices they encounter.

WHY AREN'T THERE MORE AFRICAN-AMERICAN STUDENTS IN THOSE CALCULUS CLASSES?

Not only have researchers attempted to show that African-American students experience differential treatment from teachers and school officials but it has been suggested that students, themselves, limit their access to higher level mathematics by not enrolling in these courses when they have the opportunity to do so. Data from course-taking and persistence studies shows that in high schools where African-American students predominate, only one in five students take more math than the minimum required for graduation (e.g., Dossey et al., 1988; Oakes, 1990b; Silver et al., 1995). Moreover, these same studies show that less than half of these students take mathematics beyond algebra and one in five do not take any algebra.

Although there have been reports of increased enrollments in high level mathematics courses by African-American students and reverses in tracking practices, these reports have also been viewed with skepticism. Close scrutiny has shown that these increases have occurred mainly at the beginning algebra level and have not extended to higher-level courses. As a result, there have been no dramatic increases in the numbers of African-American students choosing mathematics-based majors at the college level or entering these fields in the labor market (Patterson, 1991). In fact, some studies show that Whites continue to make up nearly 85% of the science and math majors in college (Oakes, 1990b). Other studies show that African-Americans make up only 2% of the nation's engineers and scientists, and 2% of the Ph.D.s in these areas (e.g., National Center for Educational Statistics, 1997).

Although some students do not master the prerequisite material for advanced math courses and attend schools in which these advanced courses are not offered, it is not clear why other African-American students do not enroll in higher-level mathematics courses when these courses are offered or when tracking does not prevent them from doing so.

THEY'RE POOR, BLACK, AND
THEY ATTEND BAD SCHOOLS

Given that more than 40% of all Black children live below the poverty level (Patterson, 1997), it is not surprising that they are also less likely to have access and exposure to high-quality educational resources. Moreover, because African-American students often live in poorer, urban school districts, we know that they are also less likely to have access to modern school facilities, computers, highly qualified and experienced teachers, advanced classes, small classes, and enrichment activities (Oakes, 1990b).

Are family and socioeconomic background and limited access to resources the real reasons African-American students do not achieve up to their potential or persist in mathematics? Without question, these factors do have an effect on mathematics achievement and persistence. One would be remiss to ignore the devastating effects of poverty and economic ruin in some African-American communities. Moreover, African-American students often are forced to attend schools that are unsafe and in poor condition. However, appeals to these factors are limited in explanatory scope and cannot, by themselves, account for mathematics achievement and persistence differences among students. In particular, these explanations fail to account for intragroup achievement differences and African-American student success in spite of these background factors. High achieving African-American students often come from the same communities, share similar socioeconomic backgrounds, attend the same schools and classrooms, and experience the same teaching methods and curricular practices as their unsuccessful peers.

These explanations also fail to highlight the positive contributions that many Black parents, regardless of SES, make to their children's education. African-Americans have a long history of individual and collective struggle and accomplishment—leading to significant gains not only for African-Americans but other groups as well. Black children live in communities with people who exemplify these struggles and accomplishments (Anderson, 1988). Few mathematics education researchers have examined the dynamics of family background or community-based supports to determine the ways in which students draw strength from these resources (e.g., Clewell, Anderson, & Thorpe, 1992). Several questions remain largely unexplored: What kinds of resources and support do students obtain from their families and communities? How do we explain differential achievement within African-American student groups, families, and communities? Are there explicit and implicit messages that students receive within these contexts about the role and importance of mathematics and schooling? How do students interpret and respond to their family situations and the life experiences of their parents? Analysis of interview data from students, parents, and teachers in this study suggests answers.

A CONCEPTUAL FRAMEWORK FOR UNDERSTANDING MATHEMATICS ACHIEVEMENT AND PERSISTENCE AMONG AFRICAN-AMERICANS

Explanations based on conventional studies of African-American student achievement and persistence problems in mathematics have been effective in highlighting inequities in the schools, the socioeconomic backgrounds of students, and other contributory factors. However, few mathematics education researchers have advocated appropriately complex theoretical perspectives that situate mathematics achievement and persistence outcomes in broader sociohistorical, cultural, and community contexts (e.g., Hart & Allexsaht-Snider, 1996; Jones, 1993; Knoff, 1993; Oakes, 1990b; Reyes & Stanic, 1988; Saxe, 1992).

One exception is a framework proposed by Reyes and Stanic (1988) to identify key variables that might explain intergroup mathematics achievement differences. The authors identify "societal influences—

the family, the community in which the student lives, religious institutions, the mass media, and implicit messages that result from the pattern of prevailing occupational and other societal roles held by members of a particular group"(p. 33)—as the starting point in their model and comment:

> There is little, if any, research documentation of the effect of societal influences on [teacher attitudes, school mathematics curriculum, classroom processes, student attitudes, achievement related behavior, and student achievement]. Documenting these connections is both the most difficult and most necessary direction for future research on differential achievement in mathematics. (p. 33)

This claim is supported by Schoenfeld (1992), with the additional proposal that we integrate fine-grained analyses of students' mathematical behaviors with studies of the social contexts in which these behaviors are embedded:

> [We] understand little about the interactions among [beliefs, resources, problem solving strategies, and practices] and less about how they come to cohere—in particular how an individual's learning fits together to give the individual a sense of the mathematical enterprise. . . . My own bias is that the key to this problem lies in the study of enculturation [and socialization]. . . . And if we are to understand how people develop their mathematical perspective, we must look at the issue in terms of the mathematical communities in which students live and the practices that underlie those communities. (p. 363)

Oakes (1990b), in a comprehensive review of women and minority students in pre-collegiate mathematics and science, offered another compelling call for attention to larger contextual factors affecting mathematics achievement and persistence:

> The importance of societal factors on the attainments of women and minorities cannot be overlooked. . . . Although much literature has documented the relationships of socioeconomic factors to student achievement, opportunities, and choices, less work has explored the mechanisms through which societal factors may actually have these effects. . . . Psychological research, for example, supports the idea that environmental conditions influence children's beliefs about their prospects for success and about the rewards they can expect from their efforts. . . . When individuals are placed in subordinate roles or given labels that imply inferiority or incompetence, their self-efficacy and performance are often negatively affected (Bandura, 1982). This

.... supports the notion that students respond to school in ways that seem reasonable to them, given the messages schools and larger society send them about their prospects for school success and the rewards they might expect from the hard work that success requires .... Although societal factors undoubtedly influence the educational attainments of minorities and women, these background characteristics do not operate independently of students' experiences in schools. The evidence about schooling differences . . . suggests that schools, too, respond to race, class, and gender in ways that exacerbate the difficulties of girls and minorities in science and mathematics. . . . Most likely, it is the coming together of individual student characteristics, societal influences, and schooling opportunities that is most relevant to understanding and improving the participation of underrepresented groups. Some analysts have proposed that both schooling opportunities and students' responses to schooling are influenced by the current social milieu that holds particular norms and expectations about different groups of students. If this is the case, schools' definition of individual differences and decisions about what opportunity should be provided to different students may be influenced by societal as well as educational factors. (pp. 200–202)

Unfortunately, a framework such as that proposed by Reyes and Stanic and a theoretical perspective such as that proposed by Oakes have not resulted in significant numbers of empirical studies.

Mathematics Socialization and Identity

Does the absence of such studies mean that they are not possible? Absolutely not. But if such empirical studies are to be undertaken, we need appropriate theoretical and methodological tools. Here, the focus on *mathematics identity* and *mathematics socialization* and the methods that I use to investigate them offer one such set of tools. Throughout this book, mathematics identity refers to the participants' beliefs about (a) their ability to perform in mathematical contexts, (b) the instrumental importance of mathematical knowledge, (c) constraints and opportunities in mathematical contexts, and (d) the resulting motivations and strategies used to obtain mathematics knowledge. Mathematics socialization describes the processes and experiences by which individual and collective mathematics identities are shaped in sociohistorical, community, school, and intrapersonal contexts.

Why socialization and identity? The notions of mathematics socialization (e.g., Bishop, 1988; Resnick, 1989; Schoenfeld, 1992) and identity were useful for several reasons. Socialization as an explanatory concept allowed me to account for both the sociohistorical and present-day mathematical experiences of African-Americans. In addition, socialization also highlighted the fact that the parents and community members, students, and teachers in this study were active rather than passive participants in these processes.

A focus on identity allowed consideration of the participants' definitions of what it means to be African-American in the context of mathematics learning. Prior research, as well as recent controversy (e.g., the Oakland, California Unified School Board resolution on Ebonics) suggest that some behaviors such as speaking standard English and pursuing academic achievement are perceived of and defined as "acting White" by some students and parents (Fordham, 1988; Fordham & Ogbu, 1986; Luster, 1992). Moreover, the lack of African-American role models in mathematics-related areas might send its own message. Given these cultural associations and external messages and images, one might ask: "Do some African-Americans avoid crossing these so-called cultural boundaries and, if so, what impact does this have on their motivations to excel in areas like mathematics?"

There already exists a vast literature on the complexities of racial identity development among African-Americans (e.g., Cross, 1991; Fordham, 1996; Hale-Benson, 1994; Helms, 1990; Tatum, 1997; Welch & Hodges, 1997). A focus on racial identity development is certainly beyond the scope of this book. However, the analyses presented here are informative in their own right and do make a contribution to that larger discussion.

As the analyses in subsequent chapters unfold, it will be become clear that what is called mathematics identity among the participants is intimately linked to several other identities that constitute their larger senses-of-self. First, there appears to be a close connection between mathematics identity and academic identity among students. Second, there appears to be a close connection between mathematics identity and African-American identity among parents and community members. For example, as they offered what amounted to commentaries on race and what it means to be African-American, I was able to get the parents and community members in this study to narrow their discussions to mathematics. They did so in ways that accounted for how they believed their African-American status, and the treatment they received as a result of this status, helped or hindered their participation in mathematics. I am not aware of any studies of African-American identity development that have narrowed their focus to the academic discipline of mathematics. I also know of no studies of mathematics learning, persistence, or achievement among African-Americans that have attempted to explicate the concept of mathematics identity.

Cultural and Community Beliefs About Mathematics

The notion of *community*, as used in this book, needs a bit of clarification. Those who differ or find fault with this perspective may claim that this book attempts to generalize to all African-Americans based on the study of a few. But my search is not for a one-size-fits-all explanation. Starting with the detailed analysis of the stories of a relatively small number of African-American parents, community members, and children, this book generates sound hypotheses about larger numbers of others who share their experiences.

The term *community*, as used here, does not refer to a specific physical location nor does it imply that all the participants think or act alike. It connotes the fact that the participants in this study share their African-American status and that they, themselves, have identified common sets of experiences that they attribute to this status. The term *community forces*, in my conception, includes the individual life histories as well as the shared, collective experiences of African-American parents and community members in those larger socioeconomic and educational contexts for which mathematics plays an important role. *Community forces* also describe the individual and collective beliefs and attitudes about mathematics that prevail among these parents and community members as a result of these experiences as well as the educational strategies they use to obtain mathematical knowledge.

The idea of community forces also derives partly from the work of Ogbu. When it became clear to me that factors outside the school were playing a role in the mathematical behaviors of the students at Hillside, Ogbu's work offered the initial inspiration to investigate these factors (Ogbu, 1974, 1987a, 1987b, 1988, 1989a, 1990, 1992a, 1993). Not surprisingly, my definition and use of the term *community forces* bears a strong family resemblance to Ogbu's definition. However, it differs in respects that seem to have particular explanatory power in the context of the research discussed in this book.[1]

Most important, if one is not inclined to believe that achievement and persistence outcomes are affected only by what happens in the school context, Ogbu's perspective and theoretical framework—

---

[1] Ogbu (personal communication, April 20, 1997) has pointed out that a major difference is that his work focuses on categories and groups while the work in this book focuses on the detailed analysis of individuals.

developed from comparative, ethnographic studies of various minority groups—provide some indication of which additional factors might be considered. In particular, he suggested that problematic outcomes in minority student achievement are not determined in a straightforward manner by personal background or school-related forces but also have a sociohistorical basis. Furthermore, these outcomes are constructed in complex interactions among several forces. These forces include those that emanate from the larger society—racism, discrimination, and limited access to economic opportunity—and that impinge on a minority group's collective belief system. Acknowledging the role of societal forces in the lives of African-Americans, Ogbu (1987b) identified mechanisms such as:

> [The] historical practice of denying minorities access to desirable jobs and positions in adult life that require good education and where education pays off. . . . By denying the minorities opportunity to gain entry into the labor force and to advance according to their educational qualification and ability, and by denying them adequate rewards for their education in terms of wages, American society discouraged the minorities from investing time and effort into pursuit of education and into maximizing their educational accomplishments. Since this discouragement went on for many generations, the effects have probably been cumulative and relatively enduring. Furthermore, the experience has probably discouraged the minorities from developing a strong tradition of academic achievement. (p. 318)

According to Ogbu (1987b), community forces should be implicated in school performance and achievement at least as much as those forces that emanate from the societal or school context:

> The complex and interlocking forces that affect the social and academic performances of minority children are not limited to those of the wider society, the school, and the classroom; they also include those from the minority community themselves. The "community forces" are different for different minorities and they interact differently with societal and school factors, producing different educational results. (pp. 288–289)

Ogbu defined and described four theoretical constructs that make up these community forces: *cultural models, cultural frames of reference, degree of trust or acquiescence,* and *educational strategies. Cultural models* are "people's understanding of their universe or their world, and refer to how those understandings influence the ways in which people interpret and respond to events in that universe. Cultural models ask questions like 'What does it mean to be Black in America?'"(Ogbu, 1989a, p. 11). *Cultural frames of reference* refer to beliefs about "the correct or ideal way of behaving within a culture—attitudes, beliefs, preferences, and practices considered appropriate for members of the culture" (Ogbu, 1993, p. 490). *Degree of trust or acquiescence* refers to the kinds of relationships that various minority groups have with members of the dominant group. Finally, *educational strategies* refer to the attitudes, plans, and actions that are used in the pursuit of formal education.

Taken together, these four components of community forces help explain how deep, psychological orientations toward education can develop as a result of experiences in societal and socioeconomic contexts. These psychological orientations, in turn, can shape behaviors in school contexts. Ogbu (1987b) explained the possible effects of these community forces on achievement outcomes:

> The initial term of incorporation into American society together with subsequent subordination and exploitation shape the minority group's cultural models of schooling. The latter includes the members' perceptions and interpretations of schooling, degree of reliance of schooling as a strategy for making it, relationship with the system and with White people who control it, and so on. The cultural model, in turn shapes the strategies that minorities adopt toward schooling. Now, the minority group's adaptations to minority status in the wider society, its cultural model of schooling, and strategies toward schooling form an integral part of the cultural curriculum that the minority child learns in the course of growing up in the community. This curriculum . . . is taught to the child consciously and unconsciously through culturally patterned processes and techniques by agents responsible for the child's upbringing, including the family, peer groups, religious organizations, the mass media, and role models. As the minority child gets older he or she may actively seek to acquire the adaptations, the cultural model, and educational strategies of the group. Thus, when the minority student comes to school, he or she comes with an emerging knowledge, set of attitudes, and strategies that can promote or discourage social adjustment and academic performance, depending on what the child encounters at school. (p. 333)

Ogbu's perspective has generated a great deal of debate and has resulted in both praise and criticism. He has been praised for countering widely held cultural-deficit, cultural-difference, and cultural-discontinuity perspectives by pointing out that cultural differences alone cannot explain the low achievement of some student groups, given the success of students whose cultural and language differences are similar, if not greater, than those claimed for students who do not succeed. He has also been praised for providing evidence that the antecedents of school behaviors extend beyond the school context and can originate within minority groups themselves. Some researchers have raised objections to Ogbu's perspective, claiming that it "tends to be reductionist to a position of economic determinism" (Trueba, 1988, p. 275) and that his taxonomy of minority groups "does not explain why individuals subjected to the same oppression, even from within the same ethnic group, respond differently" (p. 276).

The purpose of this book is not to offer an extended critique or praise of Ogbu's perspective. Instead, it utilizes those aspects of his work that are essential to help accomplish the primary task: understanding mathematics learning, achievement, and persistence among African-Americans.

For me, Ogbu's work on sociohistorical and community forces provides a partial explanation of academic achievement among African-Americans by focusing on disproportionate failure. Yet, there is also a need to explain success among African-American students as well as to explain differential achievement and persistence within specific content areas like mathematics. Similarly, research on mathematics achievement and persistence among African-American students that focuses narrowly on school-level and personal background factors needs to be extended to take into account issues of sociohistorical and community forces as well as individual agency on the part of African-American students and parents.

Without these considerations, the extent of our knowledge of the factors that influence mathematics achievement and persistence among African-Americans will continue to be confined to the following, which were discussed previously:

- African-American students lack the necessary knowledge and problem solving skills as demonstrated by performance on achievement tests.

- African-American students experience differential treatment by teachers and school officials, are often tracked into lower level classes, and are given access to poor teaching and instructional resources.

- African-American students come from family backgrounds and experience socioeconomic difficulties that hinder their academic achievement.

How might we begin to link broader, sociocultural, socioeconomic, and community concerns with those concerns that have particular relevance to mathematics educators interested in achievement and persistence issues among African-Americans? My own belief is that introducing concepts such as mathematics socialization, mathematics identity, and cultural models of mathematics into discussions of mathematics persistence and achievement among African-Americans and collecting the kinds of data that explicates these concepts offers one such strategy.

Given that most empirical studies of mathematics achievement and persistence among African-Americans have avoided analyses of sociohistorical and community forces and that most research on community forces has yet to focus on mathematics learning, one question addressed in this book is: *How do their experiences in socioeconomic and educational contexts characterize their mathematics socializations and affect the construction of mathematics identity among African-American parents and community members?*

In chapter 2, a partial answer to this question is offered. The discussion shows that the African-American parents and community members interviewed in the study drew heavily on their experiences in socioeconomic and educational contexts as well as their beliefs about how these experiences were influenced by their African-American status to help them form their mathematics identities. The participants' first-hand accounts of their experiences offer compelling commentaries on race, identity, and mathematics.

In my view, the most significant aspect of examining cultural and community beliefs about mathematics is being able to identify and counter those beliefs that have a potentially negative effect on African-American children. It is not difficult to imagine that where negative messages do exist, they have a historical basis and will probably be reflected in parents' and community members' accounts of their own negative experiences in mathematics-related contexts, rationalizations about their own lack of success in mathematics, and conflicts with teachers and school officials.

One consequence of these kinds of community beliefs is that African-American children might respond by disassociating themselves from the doing of mathematics as an instrumental endeavor when it appears that doing mathematics is for others. Making this claim does not discount the fact that African-American students do work hard in school and that they genuinely want to succeed. But, at a deeper, psychological level, their in-school efforts may be tempered by realities in their schools, communities, and the wider society that send mixed messages about their ability to benefit from mathematics knowledge.

It should be understood that the goal in focusing on cultural beliefs about mathematics is not to create doubt about whether African-Americans value mathematics learning as an important school subject. Neither should these efforts be misconstrued as an attempt to blame African-Americans for problematic outcomes in mathematics achievement and persistence. Indeed, prior studies have revealed that, when asked about its importance, African-Americans do rate mathematics as a highly valued school subject. Moreover, individual African-Americans have managed to achieve success in mathematics. But we know that as recently as the 1960s, African-Americans were legally denied access to employment and educational opportunities. This treatment persists. In scientific and technical arenas, where participation is based on knowledge of mathematics, there continues to be a limited African-American presence.

Given the realities of their experiences with denied opportunity, their encounters with racism and discrimination, and their often poor educations, I believe it is a matter of necessity that we examine the true meanings that mathematics learning assumes among African-Americans in the context of these experiences. Rephrased as an empirical question: Is there any evidence that participation in mathematics or the acquisition of mathematics knowledge assume diminished importance in the everyday lives of African-Americans? If not, what accounts for the discrepancy between the desire and motivation to participate in mathematics and well-documented achievement and persistence problems? Some cultural groups, most notably Asian Americans, have received great praise for their efforts in mathematics, but few researchers have attempted to investigate the evolution of cultural meanings for mathematics among African-Americans and the effect of these meanings on mathematics achievement and persistence.

Therefore, when interpreted correctly, the focus on African-Americans' cultural beliefs about mathematics is not an attempt to blame African-Americans for problematic outcomes in mathematics. Rather, it is an attempt to direct attention to their historical legacy of denied opportunity in mathematics and its relation to seemingly unsolvable achievement and persistence problems. It is also a call for further exploration by mathematics educators into African-Americans' beliefs about and responses to this historical legacy.

School-Level Factors

Examining cultural and community beliefs about mathematics among African-Americans is important. Yet, there is also a need to reexamine those school-level factors that have typically received the most attention in studies of achievement and persistence. In this book, a small number of these factors is identified, including school-based mechanisms that promote or hinder mathematics learning for African-American students; the role of teachers as agents of mathematics socialization, including their beliefs about and goals for African-American students; the role of peers in mathematics socialization and identity formation; and the ways in which classroom and curricular practices serve as contexts that promote positive or negative mathematics beliefs and identity. I examine these forces through the lenses of socialization and identity and show the dynamic and unpredictable ways in which they unfold and interact to affect achievement and persistence among Black students, not as deterministic givens.

In chapter 3, the following question is addressed: *What are the natures of school and classroom forces and how do these forces interact with larger community forces to affect mathematics socialization and identity among African-American students?*

It is no coincidence that the question couches school-level issues in their broader social and community contexts. My analysis shows that the conditions for mathematics learning and teaching at Hillside were, in fact, affected by these larger contextual forces.

At the classroom and curricular levels, I explore the dynamics and tensions involved in the negotiation of social and mathematical norms between students and teachers and among students. This negotiation reflects the fact that students and teachers are continuously involved in sense-making processes—not only in trying to understand the mathematics content and practices that they experience but also in evaluating the overall importance and relevance of these practices to their own identities, beliefs, prior knowledge, expectations, and goals.

I found that teachers contributed to this negotiation process through their attitudes toward and beliefs about students as well as their subsequent choices of mathematics content and curricular practices. These beliefs and practices were affected by several factors including teachers' own life and educational experiences, their beliefs about ideal ways of knowing and doing, their beliefs about their students' ability and motivation, their beliefs about students' parents and communities, as well as by demands placed on them by state and district curriculum mandates.

Students contributed to this negotiation through their acceptance or refusal to adhere to the prevailing social and academic norms that defined their school climate and dominant student culture. Although it appeared that a majority of students chose to adhere to a widespread underachievement norm within the school, others chose to establish their own identities and adopt goals that were more closely aligned with success.

Also discussed is how the competing norms among teachers and students, and the everyday struggle to reconcile them, had a dramatic effect on classroom practices. Some students responded favorably to the social and mathematical demands made on them but many others experienced difficulty or were not motivated to engage in the practices stressed in their classrooms. Observation data describing classroom interactions among the teachers and students at Hillside show that in-class time for teachers was often split between mathematical content issues and correcting and modifying student behavior to adhere to the demands of the chosen content and curricular practices. These conditions created classroom environments exemplifying the difficulties of both teaching and learning mathematics.

Student Success and the
Role of Intrapersonal Agency

Despite these conditions, there were some students at Hillside who were academically and mathematically successful. Although I refer to a range of dispositional factors and strategies that contributed to their success, an important, and often neglected, component was individual agency (e.g., Bandura, 1986). This agency emerged in the contexts of both the community forces and school forces that students lived with on a daily basis. A particularly important finding was the degree to which successful students recognized and responded productively and effectively to their surroundings. They did this by engaging in a kind of self-definition by opposition and resistance to what they considered to be negative influences.

Because few studies have focused on academic success among African-American students and fewer have focused on students who do well in mathematics, issues of individual agency, success, and persistence remain largely underconceptualized. Success, for example, has been defined only in terms of external measures such as grades and test scores, and persistence has been defined only in terms of course-taking patterns.

In chapter 4, the following question about successful students at Hillside is addressed: *What kinds of personal and mathematics identities are constructed among successful students and what kinds of experiences and goals shape these identities?*

The students whose interviews are discussed in chapter 4 identified many obstacles inside and outside of school that affected their conceptions of success and their motivation to succeed. Many of these students often cited teasing or ridicule from their classmates as potential barriers. Although harmful to different degrees, these taunts, at their worst, can amount to threats and challenges to the ethnic and cultural identities of these students. These taunts may also reveal an underlying belief among some African-American students that some behaviors, such as engaging in serious study or doing well in mathematics, are considered inappropriate or "White" behaviors and that engaging in such behaviors should be avoided. If this is true, successful students must make serious decisions about crossing these cultural boundaries.

Putting the Pieces Together:
A Multilevel Framework

A growing number of mathematics education researchers have identified social and cultural influences as important considerations in research on mathematics learning. What has not been made completely clear is how to integrate methods typically used to study sociocultural issues with widely used cognitive science approaches to studying mathematics learning. The individual methods employed for the research in this book—ethnography, participant observation, and use of case studies—were highly effective in addressing issues of socialization, cultural meaning, and identity. These methods were also useful in helping me uncover and interpret some of the most deeply held mathematical beliefs of African-American parents, community members, and adolescents.

The capstone of the research in this book is a multilevel, context-based framework of sociohistorical, community, school, and intrapersonal themes that I believe captures salient aspects of mathematics socialization and identity formation among African-Americans. That framework is presented as Table 1.1.

Construction of this framework was an iterative, data-driven task. The framework not only describes the contextual influences on mathematics socialization and identity among African-Americans, but it can also be used to explain, in sufficiently detailed ways, how these influences affect and characterize mathematics socialization and identity.

The top level of my framework refers to the historically based discriminatory policies and practices that have prevented African-Americans from becoming equal participants in mathematics and other areas in society. In chapter 2, the historical legacy of these practices is

TABLE 1.1
Multilevel Framework for Analyzing
Mathematics Socialization and Identity Among African-Americans:
Key Themes

Sociohistorical

- Differential treatment in mathematics-related contexts

Community

- Beliefs about African-American status and differential treatment in educational and socioeconomic contexts

- Beliefs about mathematics abilities and motivation to learn mathematics

- Beliefs about the instrumental importance of mathematics knowledge

- Relationships with school officials and teachers

- Math-dependent socioeconomic and educational goals

- Expectations for children and educational strategies

School

- Institutional agency and school-based support systems

- Teachers' curricular goals and content decisions

- Teachers' beliefs about student abilities and motivation to learn

- Teachers' beliefs about African-American parents and communities

- Student culture and achievement norms

- Classroom negotiation of mathematical and social norms

Agency and Mathematics Success
Among African-American Students

- Personal identities and goals

- Perceptions of school climate, peers, and teachers

- Beliefs about mathematics abilities and motivation to learn

- Beliefs about the instrumental importance of mathematics knowledge

- Beliefs about differential treatment from peers

brought to life in the narratives of African-American parents and community members—narratives characterized by repeated references to beliefs about differential treatment in mathematics-related contexts.

Elaboration of these cultural and community beliefs about mathematics continues in the second level of the framework. Here, the focus is on the participants' beliefs about mathematics abilities, their motivations for obtaining mathematical knowledge, their beliefs about the instrumental importance of mathematics, their relationships with school officials and teachers, and their socioeconomic goals and expectations for themselves and their children.

The third level concerns school-level factors. The primary focus is the negotiation of mathematical and social norms that occurs in African-American students' classrooms. In the classrooms that were studied, this negotiation was influenced by teachers' beliefs and choices of content and curricular practices, students' beliefs about mathematics, and the aspects of the dominant student culture of low achievement and low motivation that entered the classroom to challenge and resist the chosen classroom and curricular practices.

Finally, the fourth level of the framework focuses on successful African-American students and addresses a variety of themes that account for their success in spite of or in light of the contextual forces they encountered. These themes highlight the strength, resiliency, and agency of these students and raises questions about many of the typical assumptions about African-American students and their responses to these forces.

There is no claim that the themes in my framework describe all aspects of mathematics socialization and identity among African-Americans. Rather, these are themes that arose from an interpretive analysis of both interview and observation data. The small number of case studies from which these themes emerged are also not complete characterizations of mathematics socialization and identity among all African-Americans. These stories do, however, represent important slices and cross-sections of processes that have evolved and that will continue to evolve for each of the participants in this book as well as for the other African-Americans who shared their stories with me.

It has been said that documenting the relations between sociohistorical, community, school, and intrapersonal forces is the "most difficult and most necessary direction for future research on differential achievement in mathematics" (Reyes & Stanic, 1988, p. 33), yet, the number of studies devoted to accomplishing this task has been minimal. Typically, studies have focused on one of these contexts (usually the school), minimized attention to the others, or simplified relationships between them for ease of analysis or reporting. The depiction of these contexts presented in Figure 1.1 is consistent with

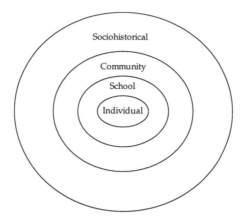

FIG. 1.1. Multiple contexts of analysis.

these simpler conceptualizations. It represents one way to organize the grain size of analysis and the scope of these contexts, but my data and analyses suggest that there is much more complexity that describes and explains the relations between these contexts.

Although my own outline of sociohistorical, community, school, and intrapersonal forces proceeded in a mostly linear fashion, a major goal of this book is to explain relations between the forces across these contexts in ways particularly useful for mathematics educators. Table 1.1 was one way to explicate the complexity—it simply listed important themes within each context. Figure 1.1 does so as well but there are problems. One problem is that it appears highly deterministic and leads to an oversimplification of the ways in which contextual variables affect mathematics achievement and persistence. In my view, this is the naive model of context that has often guided attempts to remedy problematic achievement and persistence outcomes among African-American and other underrepresented groups. The assumption behind these efforts seems to suggest that if we change the curriculum, determine the right combination of classroom activities, choose the right content, or fix some other aspect in the school context, then students will do well as a trickle down effect.

As presented, the depiction in Figure 1.1 also seems to imply that forces in larger contexts overpower those in smaller contexts and that larger contextual variables determine the fate of the individual. This is wholly inconsistent with considerations of human agency—agency that "operates within a broad network of sociostructural influences" (Bandura, 1997, p. 6).

In his social cognitive theory of thought and action, Bandura (1982, 1986, 1997) identified a key mechanism of human agency: *perceived self-efficacy*. Bandura (1997, p. 2) defined perceived self-efficacy as "beliefs in one's capabilities to organize and execute the courses of action required to produce given attainments." He further stated:

> People's beliefs in their efficacy have diverse effects. Such beliefs influence the courses of action people choose to pursue, how much effort they put forth in given endeavors, how long they will persevere in the face of obstacles and failures, their resilience to adversity, whether their thought patterns are self-hindering or self-aiding, how much stress and depression they experience in coping with taxing environmental demands, and the level of accomplishments they realize. . . . Effacious people are quick to take advantage of opportunity structures and figure out ways to circumvent institutional constraints or change them by collective action. Conversely, ineffacious people are less apt to exploit the enabling opportunities provided by the social system and are easily discouraged by institutional impediments. (pp. 2–6)

Figure 1.2 begins to unpack the levels of my framework in ways that take human agency into account. Mathematics socialization and identity formation, I claim, occur as an individual negotiates the contextual forces, opportunities, and constraints that he or she encounters and that come to bear on that individual's mathematical development.

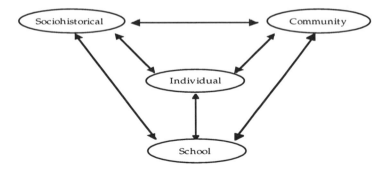

FIG. 1.2. Individual agency and mathematics socialization.

Here, the individual is not passive in their mathematics socialization. Rather, he or she is both reactive and proactive—resisting, conforming, making decisions, forming beliefs and dispositions, and constructing mathematical knowledge and identities. My reading of the extant literature in mathematics education leads me to believe that this is where most studies fall short in identifying the mechanisms responsible for producing problematic achievement and persistence outcomes as well as in accounting for mathematics success among African-Americans. The case studies and narratives that are presented in this book add texture and substance to my framework and help reveal the true complexity of the processes that lead to success and failure outcomes.

Relations between the different contexts, levels, and themes in my framework become apparent in several ways. First, narratives among African-American parents and community will highlight their individual and collective tendencies to weave together mathematics-related experiences in several different contexts. These narratives also explain how these experiences, and their subsequent responses, affected their mathematics socializations and identities. Second, when describing and explaining their classroom experiences with African-American students, the teachers often referred to demands on their teaching originating not only from within the school context but also from outside of the school. These factors included lack of parental support and the socioeconomic conditions affecting the community in which Hillside was located. Third, interviews with successful African-American students showed how they, too, wove together experiences from within their school, their communities, and their families and how they used these experiences as sources of inspiration and motivation.

In short, mathematics socialization and identity formation are, from the participants' own view, as well as my own, subject to several contextual influences. In chapter 5 of this book, additional commentary is offered on relations between these contextual forces.

In the meantime, chapter 2 begins the process of elaborating my conceptual framework and bringing to life the themes within it. I start with an analysis of mathematics socialization and identity among a group of African-American parents and community members.

2

"I Wasn't Going to Be Doing Any Math:"

Mathematics Socialization, Identity, and the Evolution of Community Beliefs About Mathematics

In this chapter, I offer an analysis of the mathematical experiences of four African-American parents and community members—whom I call Harold, Sarah, Tina, and Wendy. I surround my discussion of their experiences with discussions of other relevant aspects of their lives. I structure my analysis in this way because, as I indicated in chapter 1, mathematics socialization and identity construction are subject to a variety of influences that extend well beyond the school context.

My decision to study the mathematical experiences of African-American parents and community members came after I began my stay at Hillside Junior High. Yet, I present these data first because I believe that the experiences of adults contribute to the community contexts that students look to for messages about the importance of mathematics. Understanding the nature of African-American parents' and community members' mathematical experiences and beliefs may help us better understand the mathematical experiences and beliefs of African-American students.

I interviewed 10 parents and community members. Most were residents of Richmond, California. Eight of the 10 parents were women. Five of the ten were married. Four classified themselves as middle class; one as being on the lower level of the socioeconomic ladder; the other five classified themselves as working class. Four were in their mid- to late-20s. Three were in their 30s. Two were in their 40s and one was in his mid-50s. Their occupations included full-time student, bus driver, and dialysis technician.

All interviews were semistructured and biographical. The content of these interviews included the following topics: early school experiences, early experiences in mathematics, experiences involving education and employment, perceptions of life circumstances, perceptions of their children's school experiences, relationships with school officials and teachers, outlooks and goals for the future, and aspirations and expectations for their children. Interviews ranged from 1.5 to 4 hours and, with two exceptions, took place in the participants' homes.

The individual and collective beliefs about and meanings for mathematics among the four participants, as well as the larger group of 10, clustered around the themes listed in the second level of my multilevel framework. The second level of that framework is reproduced below in Table 2.1.

TABLE 2.1
Second Level of Multilevel Framework

Community Beliefs About Mathematics

- Beliefs about African-American status and differential treatment

- Beliefs about mathematics abilities and motivation to learn math

- Beliefs about instrumental importance of mathematics knowledge

- Relationships with school officials and teachers

- Math-dependent socioeconomic and educational goals

- Expectations for children and educational strategies

In particular, my analysis shows that the meanings given to mathematical knowledge by each of the parents and community members were consistent with traditional, folk-theory beliefs about mathematics—as a valued school subject and one in which they wanted their children to do well. But it becomes apparent here that the participants also constructed meanings for mathematical knowledge that extended beyond, and sometimes contradicted, these beliefs. These additional meanings had endured for several years and were dependent on (a) the participants' early mathematical experiences, (b) their beliefs about differential treatment and opportunity in socioeconomic and educational contexts related to mathematics, (c) the messages conveyed to them about their ability to participate in mathematical contexts, and (d) the nature of their subsequent responses to their experiences. These meanings had both positive and detrimental effects on the ways in which parents and community members' constructed their mathematics identities as well as on how they defined the importance of mathematics.

One of the more interesting findings concerned the fact that the evolution of Harold's, Sarah's, Tina's, and Wendy's beliefs about and meanings for mathematics appeared to parallel the development of their African-American identities. Moreover, the interplay between these identities had a motivating affect on all of the parents. Although one might suspect that the participants' experiences with racism, discrimination, and other barriers to their progress would have had only negative effects, the participants' responses to these experiences, and the senses of agency that grew out of it, were both positive and negative. For example, the socioeconomic and educational experiences of two of the four participants caused them to place a diminished value on mathematical knowledge in their own lives as well as in the lives of their children. The other two participants drew on their experiences as sources of motivation to reinvest in mathematics for themselves and for the sake of their children.

The first line of the title for this chapter was one of the statements that, for me, brought many of the complexities of the mathematical experiences of African-American parents and community members into sharper focus. This quote is an excerpt from an interview with Harold. It comes from a man who, at other points in his interview, was wise enough to recognize the importance of mathematics both as a school subject and for its instrumental importance, but whose early life experiences, especially in socioeconomic contexts, had so badly affected his mathematics identity that he no longer believed that he, and to some degree his 17-year-old son, could become meaningful participants in mathematics.

Of course, Harold's case is just one characterization of mathematics socialization and identity. Analysis of the additional cases show that parents were also able to invoke positive agency for themselves and their children despite their prior, negative experiences.

I believe that the small number of African-American parents and community members portrayed here, as well as those who were interviewed but not described in this chapter, represent important equivalence classes for the experiences of larger numbers of African-American parents and community members. Unfortunately, studies of mathematics socialization and identity among African-Americans are rare within mathematics education and our knowledge base of the experiences that comprise these equivalence classes is inadequate. Therefore, studies comprised of small samples are an important beginning.[2]

It should be noted that the research in this book is not intended to be a study of family socialization. Rather, it is an investigation of the mathematics experiences of a very thin cross-section of African-Americans. The manner in which the mathematical beliefs, experiences, and identities of African-American adults affect the lives of their children can only partly be inferred. Nevertheless, it does seem reasonable to suspect that African-American parents and community members respond to their experiences in ways that send implicit and explicit messages—positive and negative—about the importance of mathematics learning and knowledge to their children. I also drew on work outside the field of mathematics education to better understand the roles that families play in the schooling process for African-American children. Clark (1984), for example, contended the following:

> A family's ability to equip its young members with survival and success knowledge is determined by parents' own upbringing, past relationships and experiences in community institutions, current support networks, social relationships and other circumstances outside the home, and, most certainly [their] . . . satisfaction with themselves and with home conditions. . . . How the child comes to perceive life in the classroom will be shaped by the messages the parents provide to the child about [their] experiences with school, the [nature of the] routine communications among parents, children, and teachers, and the academic information or experience the child receives in the home which provides greater knowledge about various aspects of school subject matter. (pp. 1–5)

Despite being just one perspective among many, this characterization is useful. Very few of the African-American adults in this study could cite a history of having benefited from mathematics in ways that may have shaped a system of beliefs in which participation in mathematics was viewed as an ideal way of behaving. But because my analysis also includes cases where parents assumed a strong and supportive role in their children's education, my assumptions about the roles of families also takes advantage of the knowledge that parents are capable of invoking the kind of positive agency that is necessary for their children's success, despite their own experiences.

---

[2] Of course, analyses of the mathematical experiences and beliefs of larger numbers of African-Americans might reveal patterns not discovered here. However, even if the stories presented in this chapter are taken as idiosyncratic, it is important to report them because they may contain important information about how undesirable patterns of beliefs and actions can be broken and why well-known conditions that are thought to produce these patterns are not as deterministic as they appear.

CASE STUDIES OF MATHEMATICS
SOCIALIZATION AND IDENTITY

As suggested by Weis and Fine (1996), readers are urged to "work through" the interviewee's points as well as the accompanying analyses to gain a sense of how aspects of Harold's, Sarah's, Tina's, and Wendy's mathematics socializations and identities unfolded and how these processes affected their individual and collective meanings for mathematics.

It becomes apparent that although Harold, Sarah, Tina, and Wendy cited the same kinds of negative socioeconomic and educational experiences in their early mathematics socializations, their mathematics identities differed in important ways. Moreover, although they were able to articulate the importance of mathematics as a school subject, not all of them acted on that understanding in ways that caused them to invest in mathematics learning for instrumental reasons. The obvious question for me is: Why?

Part of the answer lies in the fact that the four participants were at different stages in the development of their mathematics identities— a process that had neither begun nor ended at the time of my study. This is first exemplified by Harold. He was one of those who recognized the value of mathematical knowledge as an important school subject and for instrumental purposes but who was unable or unwilling to act on that recognition. Much of this inability stemmed from the prolonged and devastating effects of racism and discrimination that Harold experienced earlier in his life. The narrative from a second participant, Sarah, shows that despite of and in light of her early mathematics experiences, she was able to reinvest in mathematics, develop positive beliefs about its instrumental value, and act on those positive beliefs for the benefit of her own life as well as for her children. A third participant, Tina, experienced such a traumatic early mathematics socialization that her experiences caused her to develop a seemingly fixed mind-set that she could probably never do mathematics and that mathematics was not a necessary part of her present or future life. These negative beliefs about her own abilities also affected her beliefs about what she desired for her children. Finally, readers will see that negative mathematics experiences also caused a fourth participant, Wendy, to develop a negative mathematics identity and low levels of confidence in her abilities. But, like Sarah, these negative experiences did not stop her from invoking positive agency or from reinvesting in mathematics learning, although not for instrumental reasons but for the sake of her children.

HAROLD: "I WASN'T GOING TO BE DOING ANY MATH"

Harold was a 55-year-old African-American man whom I interviewed in Richmond. He was married and had a 17-year-old son as well as other adult children. He graduated from a local high school and, over the years, had taken additional coursework off and on at a local community college. He was employed as a general contractor and he considered his standard of living to be middle class. During his interview, Harold indicated that he wanted to attend a local theological seminary because of a strong interest in biblical studies. He volunteered to participate in the study after I had initially tried to contact his 17-year-old son who was a participant in a Saturday educational program for African-American boys sponsored by a local community college. I obtained a list of participants in this program and had sought to interview some of those students and their parents. The interview with Harold and his son was scheduled for a Saturday morning but on the day of the interview his son was not there because of a prior sports commitment.

The tone of Harold's interview, from the very beginning, was characterized by deep introspection and reflection, both on his own life and on a number of other issues. Early on, I also could sense that an early life filled with negative messages about his African-American status and about his limited opportunity to participate in areas like mathematics had caused him to develop a diminished valuation of the instrumental importance of mathematical knowledge.

He first indicated these deep-seated feelings when I asked him whether he was satisfied with what life had offered him. It was clear that he was not satisfied and he indicated that he resented the treatment that he had received. I also found it very interesting that Harold was able to narrow his discussion to the area of mathematics learning and explain how his early life experiences had affected his motivation to excel in this area. It had done so to the point that he believed that he wouldn't be able to use this knowledge even if he did gain it. It was equally enlightening to learn that these experiences had lingered in Harold's memory and caused him to extend his beliefs into the life of his 17-year-old son.

Beliefs About African-American Status and Differential Treatment

I asked Harold to tell me about his experiences growing up as a young man and to reflect on those experiences both in terms of their effect on his life at that time and as points of reference for future experiences. He began by describing the social climate of the late 1950s and early 1960s, indicating that it was a time of protest for African-Americans as well as a time of rage for many who were determined to fight back against the inequities they faced. Though he indicated that he did not have any rage, he was able to indicate how those times and the treatment of African-Americans affected his life, dreams, and aspirations in very concrete ways:

DM: So, what else do you remember about your early [years]? What kind of things do you remember when you think back?

H: I just resented the fact that I was discriminated against from being able to get into the Air Force and fly jets. I wasn't aware that I had that opportunity. Though I did, I wasn't aware of it. I was more made to be aware that I couldn't more than I could. . . . I also remember a lot of the local municipal companies and major industry in the Bay Area here discriminated against Blacks—PG&E, East Bay Municipal District. I resented those things but I didn't have any rage.

I could sense that Harold was deeply affected by the differential treatment that he experienced. I could also tell that he recognized that this treatment occurred for no reason other than his race. The depth and severity of this treatment, which in may ways was the norm for African-Americans during that time, sent a strong message to Harold. This message said that his opportunities in life would be limited and that in some areas there was no reason to try:

H: Well, most of [those barriers] were racially motivated. I could see that. I guess it was the late forties, forty-eight, forty-nine, maybe even fifty. In fact as late as fifty, fifty-one that the classification of Afro-Americans went from second class citizens to you know. To have to be preoccupied with that reality I'm sure had something to do with one's desire to be an achiever. "Going for the gold" you might say. If you can't have it, why struggle for it? The whole culture at that time, it was an intimidating kind of culture that challenged an individual not to go beyond certain boundaries because there wasn't anything there for you.

Harold's comments offer strong evidence for my earlier claim that the historical legacy of denied opportunity still operates in the daily lives of African-Americans. This legacy, which has characterized a large part of the mathematics socializations of many African-Americans, can have a devastating effect on one's motivation to learn. I asked Harold if his experiences with racism and differential treatment had an effect on his educational motivation:

DM: [In your early years of schooling,] these are some of the things that you can remember?

H: Yes, those things did affect my schooling. . . . Because I saw that I was going to eventually be a laborer someplace, you know. I could see those jobs out there. I could see what aptitude and what kind of personality was required to do what was made available to me. But I didn't pursue any more sophisticated means of employment simply because I wasn't encouraged that the opportunity was there. So, I only indulged myself in my studies to the degree that I was satisfied that I could do math up to multiplication and division of fractions and decimals and that was good enough for me for what I was going to do. I wasn't going to be doing any math. To be a laborer, all it's going to require is to run a piece of machinery. . . . Because I could see that a lot of industry out there didn't require any sophisticated education to be able to perform, to earn. Like what I do now, a general contractor. It's something I never went to school for. It didn't require no formal education. I just learned most of it by observation.

"I wasn't going to be doing any math." For me, this is a very profound commentary on Harold's part. I characterize it this way because his statement makes it clear that what some might consider distant historical factors are, in fact, necessary present-day considerations in mathematics achievement and persistence among African-Americans. Harold's statement is also insightful because it adds texture and substance to my earlier claims about the parallel development of the participants' African-American identities and their mathematics identities. In many ways, Harold's comments also confirm Ogbu's (1987b) contention that:

By denying minorities the opportunity to gain entry into the labor force and to advance according to their educational qualifications and ability, and by denying them adequate rewards for their education in terms of wages, American society discouraged the minorities from investing time and effort into pursuit of education and into maximizing their educational accomplishments. Since this discouragement went on for many generations, the effects have probably been cumulative and relatively enduring. (p. 318)

In particular, Harold's comments highlight the importance of socioeconomic contexts in mathematics socialization for African-American adults, indicating that mathematics socialization is not a process confined to the school context.

Motivation to Obtain Mathematics Knowledge

Although I found that his early life experiences did not discourage him from recognizing mathematics as an important school subject, Harold's experiences with racism and discrimination did cause him to adopt a second set of beliefs. These beliefs reflected the perception that society does not reward everyone equally and that differences are based on race.

It was this second belief system that Harold referred to when talking about his lack of motivation to learn mathematics or to obtain mathematics knowledge. In what I believe to be one of his most important comments, Harold also used this belief system to account for why some African-Americans students might not be highly motivated to obtain mathematics knowledge. Although he indicated that many Black students do recognize math as an important school subject, he also suggested that their beliefs about mathematics might be tempered by several contextual factors. These include their perceptions of the economic opportunity structure and the low probability of their actually benefiting from knowledge of mathematics:

DM: In terms of some of the courses that you may have had a
        chance to take or the subjects that you were studying, did
        you see any purpose for some of those courses, like math?

H: Yeah. I saw the purpose for them and I think most kids do
        see the purpose for them and can appreciate the
        sophistication of them. But in order for one to excel at those
        things, one has to associate those things with what they
        have an opportunity to do with it. If the opportunity to do
        anything with it is not available to them, why go through
        the changes?

When comparing his early life experiences to those of African-American adolescents in the late 1990s, Harold made an interesting distinction. He pointed out that when he was a youngster he was denied both access and reward. He could not even venture into certain employment areas let alone be rewarded for his abilities. On the other hand, more opportunities than ever now exist for African-American students but many students may question whether they can expect to be rewarded appropriately for their efforts. That is, these students may believe that there is no guarantee that if one is African-American and does possess the skills, knowledge, and credentials that are typically thought of as necessary for advancement in society, that one will be rewarded equally. Harold's comments highlight the fact that although times have changed, barriers to the progress of African-Americans still exist but in a new and different form. When I asked him to comment further on today's generation of African-American adolescents, Harold said the following:

DM: Do you think [low motivation is] true for a lot of kids now?

H: I think that's true for a lot of kids now, yes.

DM: It's mainly that a lot of them don't see the opportunity attached to [math]?

H: They see the opportunity. . . . For me, all I wanted was an opportunity. The opportunity wasn't even there. So, I didn't pursue it. But what opportunity was there required so much and I satisfied that. Today's kids, I think, have the opportunity but they need more than just the opportunity. They need the guarantee.

DM: Can we guarantee?

H: Yeah, we can. If we will. I mean I can guarantee you that if you do these things, given the way the social structure is set up, there's a place for you. But you've got to set the social structure up first. . . . Which means that the Black community has to invest in itself. Then if it does that, then I can guarantee my kids "If you do this, then I got a job for you." . . . The high-achievers, the reason they're high-achievers is because they're already guaranteed . . . and they see that based on who their parents are. Their parents have pretty much guaranteed that. For example, given where I'm at, I can guarantee [my son] a job. It's not a matter of whether he can read or write or do arithmetic but can he follow basic instructions "Pick this up. Move it from there to over there. Hold this." And the rest of it is just from observation. So, you can teach a kid a trade.

In addition to offering his opinion on why African-American adolescents might not be motivated to pursue mathematical knowledge, Harold extended his comments to the larger African-American community. In his explanation, he described the same types of external forces that discouraged him from mathematics. But, in a rather interesting twist to his comments, he also described what he believed to be forces that emanate from within African-American communities themselves:

H: I think that might be true because of the fact that there's no incentives out there to excel in that area. We don't have no industry out there and the industry that is out there, they're not targeting the Black community and saying "If you go and get more math, then I can guarantee you this." But the average Caucasian may know that with math . . . he knows where his market is for what he's going to get. The average Black American doesn't know what markets there are out there for math. They're not looking at [the fact that] NASA needs mathematicians. They're not looking at who needs skilled people at math. They're not looking at Silicon Valley, that needs mathematicians. They don't know.

For me, Harold's mathematical beliefs highlight the mixed messages that may be operating to distance many African-Americans from mathematics. On one hand, there is the societal message of increased opportunity. This is a fact partly borne out by labor statistics showing that mathematical and technical areas have the largest projected job growth (Monthly Labor Review, November, 1997). On the other hand, we can find examples where industries and companies who can provide such opportunities might be sending the discouraging message to African-Americans that their opportunities in these areas are limited. For example, recent debates and controversy about the lack of availability of technically trained workers, coupled with requests by high-tech companies to recruit overseas workers, seem to ignore the possibility of attracting and training underrepresented groups such as African-Americans. If hundreds of thousands of lucrative and high-demand jobs are going unfilled while thousands of African-Americans are not pursuing or being encouraged to pursue these areas, then serious questions must be raised about why this is the case. Moreover, we can see why the kinds of responses by African-American adolescents to these messages may, indeed, be rational ones.

Expectations and Goals for Children

One of the concerns that I expressed in chapter 2 had to do with the intergenerational dialogues about mathematics that might take place among African-American parents and their children: Do the experiences of parents filter down to affect their children?

Although I could not document such conversations between Harold and his 17-year-old son, it did appear that Harold allowed his personal experiences and beliefs to affect his expectations for his son. Harold admitted that he had only minimal hopes and expectations for his son. When I asked him if he was satisfied with how his son was doing in school, Harold answered that he was, despite the fact that his son was barely a C student and struggled in his coursework. Furthermore, when I asked if he wanted his son to continue his education beyond high school, Harold was very equivocal and told me that he would not put any pressure on him to do so. Finally, it was interesting to discover that Harold seemed to discount the skills that his son could obtain in school. He offered an explanation of how his son could succeed in life without these skills and he even seemed to suggest that his son could gain access to math and science-based jobs without having any formal background in these areas:

DM: Are you satisfied with how he's doing?

H: Yeah. I'm satisfied with how he's doing. Because he's a good human being . . . and that alone will attract positive relationships. That alone pretty much has a guaranteed economic base. He can learn how to be a nuclear physicist. All [it takes is for] a physicist to take him under his wing and show him [what to do] and equate that to numbers on the board. Even though he flunked math, he can end up with a job doing physics.

DM: What are your expectations for him in terms of school?

H: My expectations of [my son]? I really don't have no expectations. I have some hopes. My expectation is that he will graduate from high school. If he doesn't, it's no big deal. I would like for him to do that. I think he will. So, I expect him to graduate from high school. I expect him to go on to college, at least on the junior college level. He's said that he was going to do that. So, I expect him to do it. It's not really a requirement for me that he do that. He can get out of high school and go to work to see what the world is all about. . . . My expectation for him is to probably be no worse than I was. Just to pass.

....

DM: So, how much more schooling do you think he needs to get along in the world?

H: How much more? I think he's had as much as he needs. Elementary school is enough schooling to get you along in society.

DM: In terms of a job?

H: In terms of general labor. Yeah. He's learned all the basic things there is like how to go out and get a general laborer's job. . . . It's no prestigious work but it's productive and a lot of those jobs pay more than specialized trades do.

Case Review

What can we learn from Harold? The naive interpretation of Harold's story is that larger sociohistorical and community forces have completely overwhelmed him.

However, I believe Harold's story is much more complex. I see a complex aspect of agency in his mathematics socialization and in the construction of his mathematics identity. It does appear that he has internalized and conformed to negative societal messages about his participation in mathematics, to the point that he believes his son cannot benefit from math either. One the other hand, Harold is also able to invoke his agency to resist these discriminatory forces— maintaining that there is something wrong with the system and the opportunity structure and firmly believing that he and his son can succeed without having to conform to this structure ("My son can be a physicist even though he flunked math"). Rather, Harold appears to adopt a strong apprenticeship model of learning, stressing the belief that it is important for his son to be a "good human being." This, in turn, will lead to someone taking him "under their wing." It is also interesting to note that although Harold was prevented from pursuing mathematics within the formal opportunity structure he, in fact, does mathematics on a daily basis in his job as a general contractor. Whether or not Harold would acknowledge this and point to this fact as his own way of gaining access to mathematics is an interesting question and one that I did not pursue. Yet, it has interesting implications for future research. Many of those who are often excluded from formal mathematics may be using mathematics in the course of their daily lives and doing so in very proficient ways. However, because of their negative mathematics socializations and identities, they may not believe that their activities are mathematical in nature. These connections between personal epistemology, socialization, and identity in mathematics among African-Americans are in need of further study.

Although Harold's views are not entirely representative of the cases that follow, his story is far from unique in its central and repeated references to African-American status and beliefs about differential treatment. Harold's beliefs about his African-American status caused him to believe that society has little to offer African-Americans.

We also saw that although Harold recognized the importance of mathematics, his early mathematics socialization—which was characterized largely by experiences with racism and discrimination—had a negative effect on his mathematics identity.

Harold's comments about today's African-American youth are also worth noting. He may have a valid point in suggesting that although the opportunity structure has changed since the time he was growing up it may not have changed enough to convince African-American youth that pursuing mathematics is worthy of their time and effort.

Harold's comments should be especially enlightening to mathematics educators because they serve as an interpretive lens through which we can examine aspects of mathematics achievement and persistence among African-Americans that are rarely studied in mathematics education—socialization and identity. Because of the complexity that comes with situating mathematics achievement and persistence in sociohistorical, community, school, and intrapersonal context, consideration of these issues is often missing in most studies of African-Americans. In my view, analysis of this complexity is necessary if we are to begin to understand how problematic outcomes, for example, are socially constructed across sociohistorical, community, school, and intrapersonal contexts.

The next case demonstrates how a negative mathematics socialization can result in an entirely different valuation of mathematics knowledge, an entirely different motivation to obtain mathematics knowledge, and an entirely different set of educational and socioeconomic goals and expectations both for parents and for their children.

SARAH: "I JUST FEEL THAT THEY FEEL BLACK KIDS CAN'T DO IT"

Sarah is a 28-year-old African-American woman whom I interviewed at her home in Richmond. She is married and has three children, two of whom are school-aged and attend public schools in Richmond. Her daughter was in eighth grade and her son was in fifth. Sarah grew up and attended school in Louisiana. At the time of the study, she had lived in Richmond for approximately 7 years. Sarah is a part-time student at a local community college and had been enrolled in a mathematics course that I taught several months earlier. In that course, she ended up as one of the top students after having started out with a great deal of apprehension about her ability to succeed. She was employed as a dialysis technician but has worked in a number of other fields including computers and administration. Her intended major at the community college was nursing.

The overall tone of her interview, unlike Harold's, was one of great expectations for herself and her children. However, she tempered these expectations by recalling the difficulties that she experienced early in her life as well as by expressing the belief that her and her children's African-American status could be considered strikes against them.

Socioeconomic and Educational Goals

During her interview, Sarah talked a great deal about the renewed value that she placed in mathematics and in her education. Her recent success in her coursework at the community college, coupled with her desire to achieve her goals of getting a better job and buying a house, had positive impacts on her mathematics identity and her overall self-perceptions. She was also motivated by the fact that she wanted to advance her status in life beyond where it was so that her children would see her as "more than just a mom":

DM: If you had to look back over your life, how would you say that life has been? Has it been fair, tough? Are you optimistic, pessimistic?

S: It's been okay. Now that I'm older, I have changed a lot. I look at life different. I have a family now so I need to start looking toward my kids instead of myself. It's been okay but I feel like I missed out on a lot of things. Now I'm trying to catch up. Like college. I'm trying to catch up now on things I missed because I want my kids to have something more than just a mom. I want them to say "My mom's a nurse or my mom's this."

DM: That's important for you to have them be able to say that? Is it good for you or good for them?

S: It's important to me. Even though my mom was just a baby-sitter. I respect her and her job because it's an honest living.

But my mom always said, "You [should] always want more for you kids." So, with me being 28 and going back to school, I hope that would encourage them that once they finish high school, they would go directly to college. Instead of the way I did, I want them to do it the right way. . . . Most people that I've run into, that I've known. Most of them just got out of high school and that's it. They didn't pursue anything else. Especially within my race. . . . For example, I have a friend of mine. We graduated from high school the same year. She's never had a job. So, she's been on the system ever since 1983. I've had four or five good jobs. I got a husband. She has never went anywhere. She has never had any motivation. When I go back home she's still in the same spot where I left her 5 years ago. After seeing stuff like that, that started to motivate me. I need to do better. I need to start advancing myself. I don't want to be "this." I want to go on a little further.

Sarah's reinvestment in her education and in mathematics could also be tied to expectations of economic rewards. It was clear that Sarah did not share Harold's beliefs about the value of credentials or about the responses of African-Americans to what they perceive in the economic opportunity structure. Whereas Harold believed that his son could succeed in life without formal education or training and, despite flunking math, "end up with a job doing physics," Sarah cited lack of credentials as one of the factors that limited her progress in life:

DM: So what's your outlook for the future?

S: Yeah, I am. That's why I finally decided to go back to school. I'm looking forward to having a very good job. I'm looking forward to buying a home. To be able to raise my kids in a better environment. Especially than where I'm living right now. My last [child], I would like for her to be raised in one house from now until high school. . . . I would enjoy an administrative position in the medical field. Something to that effect. I watch some of these people do these jobs and I think "I can do this." I just don't have the degree but I'm just as qualified as they are but I just don't have the paper.

Beliefs About the Importance of Mathematics

In terms of her mathematics socialization and identity, Sarah confessed that she did not assign much importance to mathematics in her early life. At best, she had gone through the motions of getting her school work done. She completed the minimum number of courses required for graduation but she did not develop the belief that she would actually use or need mathematics beyond the school context. Now that she was older and could look back, she expressed some regret that she did not assign greater importance to mathematics and pursue her coursework beyond algebra:

DM: Are you satisfied with how much math you learned? Did it prepare you or did you get enough of it?

S: No. No. I didn't get enough of it because, like I said, sometimes on simple equations my mind goes blank. I don't remember. No. I didn't get enough. I feel now that I should have because now I think it's more harmful to me. I didn't get enough math.

                        ....

DM: So you went to algebra in high school. Did you want to go into any other math courses or was it just your choice to stop at algebra at that time?

S: I don't know. It just never dawned on me. It was never pushed to me "Well, you've taken this algebra course [now you] need to take Geometry or whatever." It was never pushed like that. You made your schedule of what you wanted to take and that's what you took. As long as you finished your requirements for math.

                        ....

DM: Did math, in any way, stick out as being more important? Did you see it as being important in any way?

S: Not really. I knew that you had to have this [in] everyday life. But at that age, I'm thinking "I'm not going to use this." So, it wasn't of a big importance at that time.

Beliefs About Mathematics Ability and Motivation to Learn

Because of her recent reinvestment and success in mathematics, Sarah's mathematics identity and beliefs about the importance of mathematics were beginning to undergo a dramatic change. She was beginning to gain confidence in her math ability and this renewed confidence, in turn, also affected her larger sense of self. She was particularly proud of the fact that she could now help her children with mathematics and perform job-related tasks in ways that she could not do before:

DM: Do you feel different now that you're taking math?

S: Yeah. I feel differently about it altogether because I'm learning it. One other thing that I felt good about was when my daughter was doing some exponents and she was sitting there and I was like "What ya doing?" and she says "Exponents." When I came over and explained it to her, I felt so good about it. It was like "I know this, I can show her. She'll get it right." I felt good about it. It gave me a different look on the situation. It was like "Oh. This *is* what I need to be doing."

....

DM: How important is it for you now to have math or to do well in it?

S: It's very important. Because if I go into nursing, as far as medicines go. Even now in my job when patients come, you have to weigh them and you have to adjust the weights. You have an equation for when they're not getting enough Heparin. You have to figure that out by what they weigh. Here you use kilos. If a person come in using pounds in weight, you have to convert that over.

I believe this type of reinvestment in mathematics by Sarah is a key factor in helping African-American parents become more forceful advocates for their children's mathematics educations. It is critically important that these parents overcome negative aspects of their own mathematics socializations. They can do this by reconnecting to mathematics in ways that send a clear message to their children that mathematics is important and making sure that these messages extend beyond verbal exhortations.

Beliefs About African-American
Status and Differential Treatment

When I turned the focus of the conversation with Sarah to her own children, she expressed very strong feelings about the quality of education she believed they were receiving. Those feelings were mostly negative and angered her to point that she even suggested that she might send her daughter to school in another state:

DM: In terms of their schools, are you happy with [them] as places to learn?

S: Oh! I hate the schools. I really do. She's going to high school next year and there's not one, here in Richmond I want to send her to. Actually, I'm hoping she would go back to Louisiana and stay with my mom and go to high school there. Actually, her principal, he's prejudiced. That's all you can say. These schools, they're not teaching these kids and they don't have nothing for them to do. The kids are just bad. I just hate these schools. They're horrible.

Sarah's oppositional stance was related to her belief that her children's African-American status played a major role in the treatment they received from teachers and school officials. She contrasted this treatment of Black students with that received by other racial groups, whom she believed received preferential treatment at the expense of African-American children. Sarah's beliefs also exemplified her lack of confidence in her children's teachers as positive agents of mathematics socialization:

DM: [In terms of math performance] Asian students, for some reason, do well. Why do you think it is?

S: I don't think the teachers nor the school systems encourage Black kids to go in those directions. I mean, the school systems want a good football team. They want a good basketball team. . . . That kid could be failing in math. They give him a C because [they] need him to go on the basketball team. . . . You think about these kids that have graduated high school that can't even read. Can't even do a simple math problem. Only because he was a good basketball player, he made it through. . . . So, this is where [kids] put their all their energy. The classroom? They sit there daydreaming. They go to the basketball court, they're a superstar. I think it needs to be reversed. [They] need to be a superstar in the classroom. But I don't think the teachers encourage the kids to go in that direction.

....

DM: Do you have any idea why teachers might look at Black
        kids and say "We're not going to push them into math"?

S: I feel that White teachers are prone to look out more for
        their own kind and to make sure that their own kind do
        well. I feel that Black teachers don't look out for their own
        kind, don't push their own kind. And that's true within the
        Black race all together, we don't stick together, we don't
        push each other to do well. You have very few teachers that
        do that, Black teachers you know. If [they] had a choice, the
        White teacher would push the White kid, push the Asian
        kid. I feel like the kids are stereotyped—"[African-American
        kids are] not going to learn this, why push it on them." Or
        they might embarrass the kid in front of the class and the
        kid is like "Screw this, I'm not going to do this." That's
        why I feel like that. I just feel that they feel Black kids can't
        do it. . . . You might have one or two kids that can do it but
        don't even get the opportunity to do it. They don't push
        them. [They say] just because [an African-American kid
        makes an] A, so what.

Although Sarah expressed very strong opinions about teachers
and school officials, her everyday responsibilities prevented her from
visiting her children's schools more often to get a firsthand look into
what her children did there on a daily basis. This "lack of involvement"
is important to note. In the next chapter, teachers cite lack of parental
involvement in the schools as a major factor affecting African-American
students' achievement and persistence. These teachers also cited the
conflict and tension that they believed often exists between teachers
and African-American parents. Sarah's comments brought aspects of
these tensions and conflicts to life:

DM: Do you get into the schools at all or is it just kind of difficult
        to get in there in terms of your schedule?

S: Well, it's kind of difficult to get in there but what I do is I
        go see or I get their teacher to call me and I say look "If you
        ever need me, there are some times I'm off through the week
        days. You need to call me and let me know I need to come
        up there and whatever." I let them know that I am available
        to them. So they always know if they have to call, they can.
        Other than that, I make myself available to them.

DM: You do feel that you have some kind of input into the
        schools, and that they're going to listen to you?

S: I don't think so. To me, if you go up there and do all that complaining, it don't make no difference.

When I asked Sarah for additional reasons why she believed her children's African-American status made a difference in their life chances, she referred to her perceptions of the disparities that exist in the lives of some White children and the lives of some Black children. These disparities were present in Sarah's own childhood experiences and now served as motivation for her to provide her children a better life:

DM: Do you think that makes a difference because your kids are Black?

S: Oh, yes! The reason is because these White kids have everything. The color of my kids' skin, that's one strike against them right there actually. You have these parents who send their kids to camp, on ski trips. If my daughter came in and said "Mom, the school is going to go on a ski trip," I would do all I could to get that money to send her. Because when I was growing up and I saw all these White kids go to all these place and do all this stuff in school I never could go or do. It's more important for the Black children to do these things because . . . they don't have anything to keep them [out of trouble]. So what they do is they start hanging on the corner. Then the White man comes along, "Oh, look at these children." Well, of course, you done took everything because we're paying for your big house up on the hill. It is important. It's more important for the Black kids to get out and do it than any other kids, I think.

As I did with Harold, I wanted to know about the messages that Sarah might be providing to her children about education, mathematics, and their African-American status. Although Sarah indicated that she did not say directly to her children that their African-American status would affect their opportunities in life, she admitted that they may have been picking up these messages from the general environment in her home:

DM: What about in their future? Do you think [your children] will need math?

S: Oh yeah. Oh yeah, because things are changing so drastically. Yeah, because in order for them even to get a good job, they're going to have to excel very good in these courses. Especially being Black, they're going to have to excel a little higher. That's what I implant to them now.

DM: Do you make it a point, when you're talking to them about education, to let them know that because they're Black, they gotta do that much more or work that much harder?

S: Well, no. I never actually say that to them. Because I don't want them to think "Well, I'm Black, I'm not going to ever get anywhere." I never say that to them. But I kind of think they know. I kind of think they kind of know from just listening to us talk.

One of the most fascinating aspects of Sarah's narrative was her explanation of why more African-American children do not persist in mathematics. Although her earlier comments focused on the role of teachers, she was also critical of the students themselves citing their tendency to treat mathematics only as a school subject and downplaying its instrumental importance in their future lives:

DM: A lot of Black kids . . . either don't do well or they just don't stick with [math] and go on to the higher levels. . . . Everybody has a different reason. . . . Why do you think it might be? You're a parent and you have kids. . . . Why do you think that might be?

S: Because, like I said, I don't think [Black students] think it matters. It's like "Why do I have to take this math class? I'm not going to use it." I don't they think it really matters. But it does. I see now that it does. But [when I was younger] I didn't think it really mattered. I think they get the attitude "I don't want to do this." So, they do it to get a grade and that's it. I believe that's why because they don't think it matters. They don't think they're going to use it later on in life.

If such beliefs do exist, there would seem to be an immediate need to address them and an even greater need to develop strategies that promote placing greater emphasis on the instrumental importance of mathematics among African-American adolescents. These efforts should occur not only in the school context but at the community level.

Expectations for Children

Despite her comments about schools and teachers, Sarah maintained high expectations for her two school-aged children. These expectations were apparently paying off because both children were doing above average in school. Her son had recently received all B's and her daughter was a top performer who had received recognition in several areas. When I asked Sarah to explain what it was that she expected from her children, she was adamant about them doing more than the minimum and not being happy with just getting by. She was also adamant about them receiving the kinds of the skills that they would need later in their education and in life:

DM: What kind of expectations do you have [for your children]? What do you want them to get out of school?

S: As far as math goes, I want them to learn math and to be good at it . . . [so] they're not afraid of it. That's what I really want for them. As far as school. I really hope that they're teaching my kids the things they need to know to move on to the next level.

DM: What are those things?

S: You know. The basics of reading. The basics of math. To move on to your next step in math or your next step in reading.

DM: What about their grades? Do you want them to get all As? Do you want them to just pass?

S: Well, I wouldn't say I want them to get all As. But I don't want no Ds and Fs walking in the door. If they actually came in here with a D, I probably would explode within myself. But if they came and said "Mom, I cannot do any better" then I would have to go over to that school and say "Look lady, there's something wrong here. My son got a D. I need to know why he got this D. He says he can't do any better so is there a problem with you teaching him or is it a problem with him?" I just want them to do the best they can. If they don't know, that's different. But, I don't think my kids have that kind of learning problem. It would be more laziness than anything else.

Case Review

Although Sarah and Harold shared similar beliefs about the role of their African-American status in their own lives as well as those of their children, these beliefs resulted in very different responses.

Whereas Harold's experiences and beliefs caused him to disconnect from mathematics, Sarah used her beliefs as a source of motivation to develop new educational and socioeconomic goals for herself and for her children. Sarah did indicate that she assigned little importance to mathematics while in school. But because of her recent success in her community college studies, she was beginning to overcome some doubts about her mathematics ability and to develop the belief that she was capable of doing mathematics and of helping her children. Furthermore, she began to place greater instrumental value on mathematics learning and saw it as vital to both her socioeconomic and educational goals. These new beliefs and motivations contrasted with those she had while growing up, having progressed from believing that mathematics "didn't matter" and that "she was never going to use this" to believing that "this is what I need to be doing."

There is much to be learned from African-American parents like Sarah. Her story, and that of her children, is one of resiliency and agency. Sarah's prior education had only allowed her to go as far as algebra in school and her current occupation was not in a mathematics-related field. But because of her decision to reinvest in mathematics learning, she was able to make an important step toward having mathematics become a bigger part of her life. Her recent success contributed to her overall sense of self and her newly emerging positive mathematics identity. Sarah also recognized the need for her children to do well in and gain access to mathematics. The fact that she was not happy with the schools that her children attended caused her to become, to the degree that she could, an advocate for her children. Clearly, Sarah was doing her part and contributing positively to her children's academic and mathematical development—showing that African-American parents can and do have a positive effect on their children's mathematics socializations.

TINA: "IF I WAS TO GO BACK NOW FOR ANOTHER MATH CLASS, IT WOULDN'T EVEN HELP ME NOW"

Tina is a 23-year-old single mother of three girls ages 10, 8, and 3. Tina grew up in Oklahoma and moved to Richmond in 1989. She shared a house with her mother who had been disabled by a stroke and was confined to a wheelchair. Because of her early pregnancies, Tina only made it as far as ninth grade. At the time of the interview, she was attending community college as a full-time student. She was majoring in early childhood education and had plans to be a supervisor at a day-care center. When asked to describe her standard of living, Tina characterized it as "just getting by," although she was proud of herself for accomplishing what she had by the age of 23—raising three kids alone, not being on drugs, and continuing to pursue her education.

When talking about her educational experiences, Tina indicated that she did enjoy school when she was able to attend but she had only negative memories of her mathematics experiences. She characterized mathematics as her worst subject and, as our interview unfolded, it became clear that time had not diminished the effect of her experiences. In fact, Tina expressed the most negative mathematics identity among all the African-American parents and community members whom I interviewed. Because of her negative beliefs, Tina did not place much value in mathematics as a school subject or for instrumental purposes.

Throughout her interview, Tina also expressed many negative comments about the quality of her children's education. She believed that their teachers were not providing her children with a proper education and that they discriminated against African-American children. Tina also vehemently questioned the content of what her children were learning in school, preferring that her children engage in learning "their basic skills" rather than many of the open-ended, nontraditional activities that she described to me.

Socioeconomic and Educational Goals

Despite her earlier negative experiences in school, Tina had positive socioeconomic and educational goals for herself. In particular, she was committed to earning her 2-year degree and working as a day-care administrator. Although she had worked in a day-care center for a short time, she had to stop because she did not have the necessary advanced credentials. Because of this, she was now confronted with the reality that she needed to continue her education:

DM: What's your outlook for the future?

T: I want to be a supervisor of a Head Start site and that's why I'm continuing my major with early childhood development. Because, I can get my 60 units and become a head supervisor over a whole school site.

DM: Are you optimistic? Do you have positive thoughts about the future?

T: I'm very positive because I've always wanted to be a teacher especially with young children and that's what I'm going to do. I'm very sure of that.

DM: What was your motivation for enrolling in school?

T: Because I could not go back to work as a child development
        teacher unless I went to school as an early childhood
        educator. That was the reason that I had to stop working. . .
        They told me that I couldn't continue because I didn't have
        any units. . . . I kept putting it off to the side and wanted to
        do other things. So, I don't know, something happened one
        day and I just did it.

Beliefs About Mathematics Ability and Motivation to Learn

Tina's early mathematics socialization was characterized by many
negative experiences. She was confined to remedial mathematics
courses and spoke about mathematics teachers who punished students
by having them "write sentences" or stand in the corner if they did
not answer questions correctly. Tina characterized her experiences in
her mathematics classrooms as "boring" and not "fun." These
comments helped explain why she began to disconnect herself from
the doing of mathematics very early on. Tina epitomized her early
mathematics socialization by recalling her experiences with one of her
teachers:

DM: When you think back on it, [what do you remember about
        your classes at school?]

T: Math was a drag because of our math teacher. . . . He made
        us write sentences. More sentences than math. . . . He told
        us to go up to the board and do a math problem and if we
        didn't get the problem all the way correct, then we had so
        many sentences to write. So, all I could [remember] was
        me writing more sentences than doing math.

                            ....

DM: Was math interesting?

T: No. . . . He wasn't a fun teacher. He didn't make math
        interesting to us. It was very boring. Very, very boring. If
        he made it interesting to us, it wouldn't have been so bad.
        But he didn't make it interesting to us. Most teachers will
        make math fun. . . . He didn't. We could only talk so much
        in math and then we had to be quiet. It was just boring. A
        boring classroom is not fun.

                            ....

DM: Do you think you could have gone further or did you want to go further?

T: No, not with him I didn't. . . . He just wasn't a challenging teacher.

....

DM: What were your favorite and your worst subjects or the ones you didn't like?

T: My worst subject? It was math actually. Because, in a way, he made it seem like things were hard. He would explain it to us and then he wouldn't explain it to us. He would tell us one thing and then turn around and tell us something else. So, we were like confused. If we asked questions, either we were writing sentences or standing in a corner.

Tina's negative feelings about mathematics seem to intensify as she got older. She did not consider it even remotely possible that she could do mathematics, even at this stage of life:

DM: How much confidence did you have in your math ability? Did you think you were good at it back then?

T: I don't know what happened. . . . I reached the point where I just didn't care. So, it didn't matter to me whether or not I passed anything. I mean ... I wanted to do the math. I don't know, it just didn't matter to me whether or not I did it.

DM: Do you think you got enough math?

T: I think I'll do okay for now. If I need more, then I have a thick math book over there. In terms of going back for another class, I wouldn't do it. I just wouldn't do it. I think now if I was to go back now for another math class, it wouldn't even help me now.

Despite reinvesting in her education and developing new socioeconomic goals, Tina could not change her beliefs about mathematics or attach any primacy to it. She indicated that a part of the reason for this was that her teachers spent little time or made little effort to stress the importance of mathematics in broader contexts or for its instrumental value. Having no reason to value mathematics, she did not do so:

DM: Back when you were in school, [did math seem] important
          at all?

T: [My teacher] didn't make it seem that important. To me, it
          was just another class. It was because that's the way he
          made us think. He made us think that math was not
          important ... most of the students would say "I don't care.
          It don't make me no difference." So, I would tell him and I
          would let him know I didn't care. "Fine, you want to give
          me an F. You want to fail me. Do it. I don't care. Because I
          don't see why we're here anyway." But that's just the way
          he made me feel. . . . He didn't come at me making me
          think that math is what I needed. Math is what I should
          have. Math should be a very important part of my life.

DM: Okay. Did anybody else stress math to you? Outside of
          school or any other kind of teachers or counselors or
          anything?

T: No. Our counselors in school . . . the [only] time that they
          had stressed math to me is when they were changing my
          classes over. They were taking me from the special ed.
          classes and putting me in the basic math classes. That's
          when they stressed the math to me. I pushed that issue
          because I told them I wanted to be taken out of the special
          ed. class and I wanted a basic math class. That's the reason
          they put me in there. They told me before they put me in
          the class that they didn't think I was ready. I told them I
          didn't care, I wanted to go anyway. . . . For a while, I was
          okay. Then after a while, I didn't care anymore. It didn't
          matter.

Although she expressed overwhelmingly negative sentiments
about her own mathematics ability and a lack of motivation to learn
mathematics, Tina's overall beliefs about the importance of
mathematics were actually a bit more complex. On one hand, she was
discouraged at her own lack of success in math and indicated that she
had no interest in learning more math. On the other hand, Tina felt
disappointed that she could not be of more help to her children. She
expressed great frustration in this fact and it was clear that her negative
mathematics identity had an effect on her overall sense of self,
particularly on her beliefs about her role as a mother:

DM: What about now that you're back in school. Do you think
          that math is important?

T: I feel math is important but it just won't work with Tina, I don't know why. [But] I want [my children] to know math . . . I do want them to know math very much because I do feel math is a very important part in the subjects and I don't know what's wrong with Tina that she can't get it, but I want them to know math.

....

DM: If you didn't have to take [math for your current coursework] would you take it [on your own]?

T: No. I'm not taking it again. But one good thing about it is I didn't get the division at first, but now it's starting to come to me. I've been able to help [my daughter] with her division. For a while, I wasn't able to help her with her division. . . . It really frustrates me when they come to me and they say "Mom, we have math and we can't do this and we can't do that." [I have to tell her] "But mom doesn't know how to do it either." So, I have to stop and I have to think sometimes. I guess I can help you. I guess I can try. . . When they have their own children and one comes to them, they won't have to say "Oh, well momma can't help you with this because I don't know how." They'll be able say "Come on, let's sit down and I'll help you." If it's math, English, whatever, they'll have no problem with helping their own children.

Relationships With Teachers and Beliefs About Differential Treatment

Like Harold and Sarah, Tina talked a great deal about the role of her African-American status in her life experiences. At one point during her interview, she recalled the reactions that many White students and parents had toward African-American students:

DM: You mentioned that [when you were going to school, the schools were predominantly Black]. Were most of the teachers Black?

T: They were mixed. But that was the good part about it because the teachers were mixed. The school was [almost] 100% [Black]. The few White students that were there, most of them would get up and walk out. Because the school was so Black.

DM: So [the White students] felt uncomfortable?

T: I don't know if they felt comfortable or if they didn't feel
         comfortable. Half of the White students that were there,
         most of them did get up and walk out. . . . With it being so
         prejudiced, a lot of the parents did have their children either
         in Christian schools or they were in private schools. Because
         the public schools had more Black kids than anything.

Tina extended her beliefs about racism and differential treatment
into the lives of her children and drew on these beliefs to explain
problematic interactions between her children and their teachers:

DM: Which school do [your daughters] go to and what is the
         school like?

T: [Now they attend Lawson]. . . . The last school they went to
         was [Villa Elementary] in North Richmond. . . . [Lawson]
         is, I don't know, [Lawson] is kind of prejudiced against
         Black children as far as I'm concerned. . . . I think [Lawson]
         is very much prejudiced against Black children. . . . Because,
         they criticize them more. They criticize Black children more
         than anything. They explain things to them less than they
         do other children and they let them do less. I feel that they
         are very prejudiced.

DM: Are most of the teachers Black or White?

T: White. It's probably one Black teacher there.

In the course of talking about her experiences with her children's
teachers, there were repeated references and challenges to the content
to which her children were being exposed and to the activities in which
they were expected to engage. Tina expressed a firm belief that her
children were being handicapped by differential treatment based on
their African-American status and she strongly considered home-
schooling them:

DM: How are [your children] doing in school?

T: At this point, they're doing okay. They could do more. They
         don't have as much homework. I would like to see more
         homework, yes. The homework that they have are like
         newspaper articles. Especially her. The child has more
         newspaper articles than anything. She don't bring home

no English, she brings home no science. . . . Where's the English homework. Where's the math homework. Where's the science homework. Where's this stuff at. I don't see it. Where's the art homework. I never see art. Never. I know that they're supposed to be doing it. I don't see them working on their punctuation marks. I don't see them working on none of these things . . . What are they supposed to work on in fifth grade. They don't do none of these things . . . To me, the schools are not normal. That's why I say, I don't understand what these kids are learning in school. . . I just don't understand what they're getting out of school anymore.

. . . .

T: I can see why the majority of the parents are taking their kids out of school and putting them on home studies. They go to school. What are they learning? I mean, my daughter has been writing now, for about a week and a half, to 10,000. She started from 1. . . . The teacher's been having them write from 1 to 10,000. . . . She's got a stack of papers that thick. I don't see the purpose of them writing. What are they learning in school? . . . So, I go up there and I ask her "What is the purpose for all these numbers?" She tells me "Good handwriting." . . . Well, how is this teaching them good handwriting? What's the difference in them writing the numbers and them writing in cursive? What does this have to do with each other? . . . They're so far behind in a lot of things. They're just not caught up with the fractions yet. I haven't seen one time that this child has brought fractions home from school. . . . I don't understand the point of all of these 10,000 numbers. What has it got to do with math?

Expectations for Children

Tina appeared to express conflicting sets of expectations for her children. To me, this reflected the mixed feelings that she had developed about education and mathematics. In one part of her interview, she expressed the belief that her children could be doing better than they were doing in school:

DM: Okay. Are you satisfied with their work, where they're at in school or do you think they can do better?

T: I think they can do better. Yeah. I think [my oldest daughter] can do better in her math. I think [my younger daughter]

can do better. I think they could do better in a lot of the
things. What's important to me right now with them, what
I really want them to get into now is the math, the English,
the reading, the writing. Those are the main things that I
really want them to get into now. . . . If they would just
teach the kids the four main important parts, then it
wouldn't be no problem. They're not teaching them the real
important parts.

In another part of her interview, Tina, much like Harold, expressed
very low expectations for her children and indicated that she avoided
putting pressure on them to succeed:

T: I don't expect a whole world out of them and I tell them "I
        don't expect no more than what you can do. Don't overload
        yourself with something you know you can't do. If you
        know that you can't do something, then don't force yourself
        to do it. Have someone to help you, that's fine but don't
        force yourself to do something that you know you can't
        do." If they graduate, then okay, I'm happy. If they don't
        make it to graduate, then I'm still fine with them because
        they're my children and I'll accept it either way it goes
        because they still have time. They have a lot of years coming
        up and there's no use rushing now.

DM: Do you expect them to be straight A students, average
        students?

T: No, I don't expect them to be straight A students. They'll
        get some Fs, they'll get some Ds, some Cs. They're normal
        persons. Hey, I ain't met a perfect person yet on this earth.

                                ....

DM: How far do you want them to go in school?

T: I don't care if they just go through the vocational training
        and take up a training. . . . Get a job. . . . So, vocational
        training is fine. If they want to go to college [that's fine] but
        I ain't gonna make them do something that they don't want
        to do. I'm not going to say "You're going to college because
        I said you are and that's what I want you to do."

Finally, in a later portion of her interview, Tina again seemed to
contradict her earlier comments by talking about the instrumental
value of schooling and the fact that she would like her children to
recognize this value as well:

DM: You said that you were not really pleased with [your children's] schools and the teachers?

T: No, I'm not. I wanted to take them out of school and put them on home-study but then again, I don't. I want them to stay in school because I would like them to graduate. I want them to get more than what I got out of it. I don't want them to think that school is bad. I want them to go and to know that going to school is a big part of your life. I would prefer for them to be in the schools than to be in the streets. When they're at school, I know where they're at. I'm not worried about them being on corners. That's why I tell them "School is the biggest part of your lives right now because you're young. . . . Staying out of school, dropping out of school is not going to help you at all. Later on, you'll see why and you'll understand why. When you get out there and you try and get you a job you see it's not going to work because you don't have a diploma. [With only a] general education, they're going to slam the door in your face. Because that's the first thing they're going to ask you: 'Did you go to school, did you finish, do you have a diploma?' The worst thing you can tell them is no."

Case Review

Like Harold and Sarah, Tina's early mathematics experiences had a lasting impact on her mathematics identity. Of all the participants, she developed the most negative feelings about her mathematics ability and the most negative mathematics identity. Her early mathematics socialization, which was somewhat brief because of her pregnancies, had affected her to the point that she no longer believed that she could learn mathematics and she developed little motivation to do so. Although her children were enrolled in elementary school and were learning only basic math, helping them proved to be too formidable a task for Tina.

In many ways, Tina's overall life circumstances—raising three children alone, caring for a sick mother, being dismissed from her job because of lack of credentials, experiences with racist classmates— could have overwhelmed her. If her mathematics identity and expectations for her children were the only clues, it might have been easy to conclude that this was, indeed, true. But there was much more complexity to Tina's story.

It is particularly important to consider Tina's mathematics socialization and the development of her mathematics identity in context. As pointed out in chapter 1, mathematics socialization and identity formation among African-Americans are affected by factors that extend well beyond the school context. For example, Tina, in many ways, may be representative of large numbers of young African-American mothers—and other mothers as well—who must take on the responsibility of raising children at an early age. Their children, and perhaps not their education, necessarily become the primary focus in their lives. This certainly changes the nature of the educational and mathematical socialization process for these women. Schools and teachers may not be equipped to deal with these young women in ways that make them feel like regular students or in ways that allow them to gain access to coursework that can help them later in life. Like Tina, they may be confined to remedial tracks and be forced to deal with teachers like the one just described—a teacher whom she described as boring and not able to make math interesting, relevant, or important to her life. As we saw throughout Tina's narrative, this had a devastating effect on her overall sense of self and on her mathematics identity. Because of these experiences, she gave up on mathematics early and never recovered. Luckily for Tina, she did not completely give up on her education and she did establish positive socioeconomic goals.

Unfortunately, the results of Tina's negative experiences did appear to have devastating consequences for her children. The most disturbing aspect of Tina's narrative was the fact that she did not have very high expectations for her children. In fact, her experiences caused her, like Harold, to confess that she "doesn't expect a whole lot out of them." Moreover, she did not possess even the most basic mathematical skills that would allow her to help them.

WENDY: "IF THE TEACHERS THOUGHT WE COULD BE MORE THAN GARBAGE COLLECTORS AND BUS DRIVERS"

At the time of the interview, Wendy was a 38-year-old married mother of three girls who were 10, 13, and 17 years old. Wendy lives in her own home that is located in a middle-class, ethnically diverse neighborhood. She has lived in Richmond for most of her life and attended elementary, junior high, and high school there. Her two younger daughters attended school in Richmond but her oldest daughter attended a well-regarded high school in a nearby city. Wendy is a bus driver for a local transit agency. She has had this job for 13 years but has also worked at a number of other jobs including deputy sheriff. Her husband was 57 years old and is employed as a counselor at a rehabilitation center. Wendy was also attending school part time at a local community college. Her intended major was psychology. When she was in her early 20s, Wendy attended California State University for 2 years but left for personal reasons. She agreed to participate in the study by signing her name and phone number to a solicitation flyer circulated at the community college.

Wendy's interview was somewhat somber in tone, reflecting the resentment she had for many of her past life experiences. For example, she talked about her regrets of having to leave college earlier than expected. Wendy also talked quite a bit about the racism and discrimination that she believed she experienced in school, especially from her White teachers whom she characterized as unconcerned about African-American students. In Wendy's opinion, these teachers had very low expectations for African-Americans and believed Black students were only capable of being "bus drivers and secretaries." Wendy's experiences appeared to carry over into her adult life and she admitted that they had lowered her self-esteem.

Wendy's mathematics socialization could be characterized as negative but there were signs that her mathematics identity was undergoing a slow change, especially her negative beliefs about her ability. Although she made it to geometry in school, Wendy commented that she did not understand much of her coursework and that at some point, she gave up and no longer had the motivation to learn. She recalled that she received many negative messages about her abilities from her teachers and she was very upset that the African-American students in her classes were all put "over in the corner and not allowed to learn."

Despite her negative experiences, Wendy seemed determined to reinvest in mathematics learning. But, rather than for her own sake, she did so mostly for her children. She did this because her beliefs about racism and differential treatment also extended into her children's lives. But rather than passively respond to the treatment of her daughters, she invoked her agency and became a strong advocate for them. Specifically, she told me that she wanted to make sure that her daughters gained access to college-track mathematics despite attempts by her children's teachers to place them in remedial classes. In fact, because of Wendy's agency and advocacy, all of her daughters were enrolled in advanced math classes and were doing very well— her youngest having earned all As in the most recent grading period, her middle daughter a 3.5 grade point average, and her oldest daughter a 3.0.

Socioeconomic and Educational Goals

I asked Wendy to reflect on her life experiences as well as her reasons for re-enrolling in college. She responded by saying that she had made her share of mistakes in her earlier life and that these mistakes had cost her opportunities. She was now attempting to make up for these losses. Her desire to be more "than a bus driver" indicated that she felt, to some degree, self-conscious about her status in life and that additional education may be one way to move ahead:

> DM: What was your motivation for enrolling in school?
>
> W: I was supposed to start when my youngest was 5 and something happened and I didn't. I always wanted to go back. Well, I'm ready to learn now. I'll put it like that. I went to college when I was 18. I did it because of my parents, not because of me. And now I'm doing it for me and I think it's something else out there in life other than being a bus driver.
>
> DM: What about future plans for schooling in terms of either beyond what you're doing right now or how far do you expect to carry your schooling?
>
> W: Right now, I'm just looking forward to a B.S. I want to transfer from [the community college] to a state [school] or university, whatever. . . . As long as I could keep going. Whether I get the degrees or not, that's not important. It's just the education.

Beliefs About African-American Status
and Differential Treatment

Wendy's school experiences were largely characterized by traumatic experiences with racism and discrimination. As with Harold and Tina, these experiences had a negative effect on both her larger sense of self and her mathematics identity. During our discussion, Wendy became very upset when talking about the actions of her teachers, particularly when she talked about the low expectations they held for African-American students:

> DM: What was school like when you think about it? High school. Junior high. What was it like?

W: Thinking back, school could have been better if I had paid more attention. . . . Like I said, back then the teachers wasn't concerned about us. Not that they are too much now. But they wasn't concerned about us [Black students] that much. So, it was like we sat back in the corner and if you picked up something, you did. If you didn't, you didn't. And I didn't pick up. I was one of those type students that I needed to be worked with and I wasn't.

                ....

DM: What about the quality of the teachers? Do you think they were good teachers?

W: I feel if they were good teachers, they wouldn't have set us over in the corner and not let us learn. They wouldn't have just passed us through.

DM: So, some of their actions were kind of deliberate, you think?

W: I think so. I think because they had to come into a Black school or because they integrated their children with ours. I think, this is my own personal thoughts, I don't think they cared for that too much.

DM: Were most of your teachers White?

W: Most of them.

                ....

DM: I guess now you can sort of put all this together. When you look back on it, are you satisfied with the education that you received?

W: No. I think if I was prepared more in high school, I probably would have stayed when I was at State. But because I wasn't really prepared it was more easy for me to drop out. . . . But I think if the teachers thought we could be more than garbage collectors and bus drivers and prepared us for more than that, then we could. . . . It was like you took typewriting because we was all going to end up being secretaries.

It is these kinds of in-school messages and experiences that I identified in chapter 1 and that I claim have characterized mathematics socialization for many African-American parents and adults.

Beliefs About Mathematics
Ability and Motivation to Learn

When I asked Wendy to reflect on her early mathematics experiences, I quickly learned that she had developed a very low level of confidence in her abilities. Although she went as far as geometry in high school, she told me that she did not fully understand what she was doing and, after a certain point, she pretty much gave up:

DM: What was your favorite and your best subject?

W: I tell you, it wasn't English and math that's for sure. . . . Math, because I just didn't understand it. English, because I don't think it was pushed on me enough. The importance of it.

....

DM: Was the math part challenging or was it easy?

W: I guess it wasn't a challenge or easy because I didn't understand it. But I passed it, but I don't know how. I mean, I got a C out of the class but before I went back to college, I couldn't have told you anything about algebra. And that was a geometry class.

....

DM: How confident were you in your math ability?

W: I wasn't confident at all. . . . Well, as you know, as you go further along in math, if you don't catch that first step you can give up on them last ones. So, after I was lost on the first part, I knew it was downhill from there.

Because of the nature of her in-school mathematics socialization, Wendy also gradually developed beliefs that caused her to assign very little importance to mathematics:

DM: [When you were in school,] was math relevant at all? Did you see yourself as saying "I gotta have math. I gotta learn it. I gotta do it."

W: I always knew school was important and whatever you learned you would have to use it sometime in life. So, I guess it was important to a point. Relevant, important to a point.

DM: But it wasn't a major big deal?

W: Not after I couldn't get it.

Demonstrating positive agency even in the face of these negative experiences, Wendy made a major decision to reinvest in mathematics. Despite her prior mathematics experiences and negative feelings about her ability, Wendy was enrolled in a prealgebra course at the time of the study. More important, she had experienced some degree of success, earning B grades. Yet, even her short-term success was not yet enough to counterbalance the feelings she had developed over the years. She made it a point to mention that she wanted to achieve at a C level or higher so that she would know she "wasn't wasting my time":

DM: Are you confident in your ability now?

W: No not really. I'm trying but I can't say I'm good. I'm trying real hard.

DM: So, you're still not so confident? Why is that?

W: I said if I got anything lower than a C, then I wasn't going to go back because I didn't want to waste my time or their time. But I didn't, so I can go on .... That's how I'm taking this semester. If I don't do good, then I know I'm wasting my time and I'm not going back.

Although Wendy continued to suffer from low self-confidence about her mathematics ability, there was an important motivating factor that seemed to indicate that she would not be willing to give up as easily in the past—her children.

DM: If you didn't have to take math right now, would you take it? Would you have gone out on your own and said "I need math. I'm going to sign up for it."

W: I think I would have because of my children.

DM: So, your children would have been one of your motivations?

W: That would have been my only motivation.

Like all of the parents whom I interviewed, Wendy's overall sense of self was greatly affected by her mathematics identity. Her oldest daughter was enrolled in precalculus and her next oldest daughter was enrolled in algebra; Wendy was saddened by the fact that she couldn't help them with their schoolwork. She indicated that her youngest daughter would soon be going to middle school and she wanted to be able to help her. She wanted to do this so that her daughter would not be "like her mom":

> DM: What about the fact that you're taking this math class? Now that you're back in math, do you look at [your children] and say "You guys have to have it" or is just not really any relationship between what you want in math and what they want?

> W: When I look at my math class, I look at my oldest one and just feel a little bad that I wasn't able to help her.

> ....

> DM: So, how important do you see math as being now?

> W: I see math as important now because of my daughter. My oldest one is in math analysis and I wasn't able to help her at all. Once she got to algebra, I was like "you're on your own." So, she had to learn it on her own. My middle daughter, she's in algebra now and she's on her own. I find it important because I have to help my children. Especially my baby because she's going into that. So, it's real important now. . . . I don't want her to be like her mom.

Expectations For Children

Wendy maintained fairly high standards and expectations for her children. Each of her daughters was a good student but Wendy was still not satisfied. Rather than focusing solely on the actions of teachers, Wendy also held her children accountable for making school a priority in their lives:

> DM: The fact that you've come back to school, has that influenced in you in terms of their schooling, wanting more for them or wanting them to go further at all? Is there a relationship?

> W: No, because I always wanted them to go further. Whether I went back to school or not. That they should do it regardless.

> ....

> DM: Are you satisfied with their schoolwork, the grades they bring home, how they're doing in school?

W: My two oldest ones. No. . . . I think they can apply
            themselves a whole lot better than what they're doing. . . .
            I think they let their mind wander to what everybody else
            is doing instead of on what they should be doing.
            Sometimes I don't think they put school as an important
            subject on their life.

DM: What do you accept as doing a good job or what would
            make you happy?

W: On their grades, I accept Bs. I don't like Cs because I know
            they could do better. But Bs, I accept those with gratitude.

Relationships With Teachers
and School Officials

As was the case with the other parents whom I interviewed, Wendy
cited the same type of differential treatment that she received in school
as being present in her children's schooling. For Wendy, recognition
of this treatment only invoked a strong sense of agency. She was
adamant in stating that it was her responsibility to step in as an
advocate for her children because the schools are only going to "go so
far":

DM: Okay. What kind of comments do [your children] make to
            you about their schooling or them being in school?

W: How school is difficult. How teachers don't like them. How
            teachers are prejudiced.

                          ....

DM: Are you pleased with the schools as places to learn for your
            kids?

W: Yeah, pretty much. I know that the school and the teachers
            are only going to go so far. So, I know I have to take that
            extra step or encourage them that much more or holler at
            them that much more.

Wendy substantiated her claims about prejudice and differential
treatment by referring to one teacher in particular—a teacher with
whom two of her daughters had bad experiences and with whom
Wendy and her husband had numerous confrontations. When I asked
Wendy if she could recall any specific incidents or patterns of behavior

that she found inappropriate, she talked about the tracking that this
teacher tried to impose on her daughters:

DM: Is there something that sticks out that maybe you
remember?

W: I've always had to go up there and redo all their classes
because she's put them all in low-level classes.

DM: Even though they were doing well?

W: Even though they were doing well. And [my youngest
daughter is] getting a 4.0 every semester and I bet you a
dime to a dollar I'm going to have to go up to the junior
high and do the same thing for her. . . . It seems to me like
she puts all the African-Americans in low classes when they
leave her class. When they go to junior high, she makes
sure that they're in low classes.

Beliefs About Instrumental Importance of Mathematics

I also asked Wendy to comment on the fact that large numbers of
African-American students underachieve and do not persist in
mathematics. Her response was closely aligned with those of Sarah,
Wendy, and Tina—citing teachers and differential treatment in schools
but also being critical of African-American communities and parents
themselves. Wendy sternly chastised African-American parents who
did not recognize and stress the importance of mathematics to their
children:

DM: When you look at all the different student groups, African-
Americans, Whites, Asians, Latinos, [it turns out that]
African-American students, for whatever reasons, seem to
have lower scores starting early in school and they also
[have lower persistence rates in math]. They don't go into
the higher courses. You're a parent and you have African-
American kids and you've gone through school. Why do
you think that might be that those kids are just not sticking
with math or don't do as well?

W: I don't think the parents put emphasis on it enough. It's
with the parents. I don't know for sure but I don't think if I
had stressed math [for my children], the counselors or the
teachers wouldn't have did it. So, I think it's the parents
that have to stress the importance.

DM: Do you think the parents just don't know how important it is?

W: I think the parents know. I think they know but a lot of parents are just so into letting a child be a child instead of preparing them for their future that they don't push it as hard. I think that they know that their child should take more than algebra but a lot of parents say "Well, the counselor said this and the counselor said that and my teacher said this." I don't think that they realize that counselor or that teacher is White and they're not that concerned about your Black child as you should be.

Case Review

Wendy's story, like each of the others already presented, is important because it highlights the recurring belief that some African-Americans have about the role of their African-American status in their mathematics socializations. Wendy's fragile mathematics identity was almost certainly a direct result of her negative, in-school mathematics experiences. Despite having led a relatively successful life, reenrolled in college, and raised three young daughters who were all doing very well in school, the sting of her early mathematics experiences had not worn off. Yet all was not lost. Although Wendy's weak mathematics identity caused her to have a low level of confidence in her mathematics abilities, she did manage to reinvest in math, construct new socioeconomic and educational goals, and maintain high expectations for her children. In fact, her children were the primary source of motivation for her reinvestment in mathematics.

Wendy's story shows that African-American parents are not passive in their mathematics socializations. They are active agents who can and do respond effectively and productively to their experiences. Wendy, like Sarah, was able to invoke a high level of positive agency. Moreover, unlike Harold, Wendy did not let her own negative experiences carry over into the lives of her daughters.

DISCUSSION

One of the basic contentions of this book is that to better understand mathematics achievement and persistence among African-Americans, it is necessary to examine the natures of their mathematical experiences in sociohistorical, community, and school contexts as well as how their mathematics identities are shaped by forces within these contexts. My analysis of the narratives in this chapter was an attempt to show why the historical legacy of differential treatment in mathematics-related contexts is an especially important consideration in mathematics socialization and identity construction among African-Americans. I showed how aspects of this historical legacy unfolded and operated in the daily lives of Harold, Sarah, Tina, and Wendy.

As I indicated in chapter 1, specifying the exact nature of how mathematics socializations and identities among African-American parents are implicated in the mathematical development of African-American adolescents is a complex task. Understanding the nature of parents' and community members' mathematical experiences is a difficult task in its own right. Nevertheless, the case analyses presented in this chapter add to our understanding of these complexities. The participants' stories inform us about the kinds of mathematics socializations experienced by African-American parents, the kinds of mathematics identities they construct in response to these experiences, and the role that community beliefs about mathematics play in shaping the out-of-school contexts that African-American students look to for messages about the importance of mathematical knowledge.

First, despite having similar experiences and expressing similar beliefs, no uniform characterization of mathematics identity emerged among Harold, Sarah, Tina, and Wendy. But their differing mathematics socializations and identities were equally complex. A major factor that differentiated Harold, Sarah, Tina, and Wendy was the manner in which they responded to their experiences and invoked aspects of their individual agency. The nature of this agency depended on the degree to which they developed positive or negative mathematics identities and valuations of mathematics and reinvested in mathematics learning either for themselves or for their children. As a result of their economic situations or a desire to advance their positions in life, some of the parents and community members found it necessary to train for new careers or regain lost opportunities from the past. This now made mathematics a necessary and important part of their lives. Moreover, newfound success in mathematics among some of the participants influenced the ways in which they saw themselves as learners of mathematics and also affected their expectations for their children. On the other hand, some parents were unable to overcome their negative mathematics experiences. They attached little importance to mathematics, had little confidence in their abilities, and believed that differential treatment in mathematical contexts was a major barrier. Because of these beliefs and experiences, they simply gave up on mathematics. These considerations aid in our understanding of how and why the participants regarded mathematical knowledge in the ways that they did.

Second, Harold's, Sarah's, Tina's, and Wendy's mathematics socializations and identities affected their expectations for their children. Unfortunately, these expectations were not consistently high. There was a clear line of division among parents who, themselves, had reinvested in mathematics and those who did not. Parents like Wendy and Sarah, who had reentered and experienced short-term success in mathematics, assigned great importance and primacy to mathematics and had high expectations for their children. Other parents like Harold and Tina, whose experiences had discouraged them from learning mathematics and left them with mostly negative beliefs, were more inclined to expect only the minimum levels of achievement from their children.

These varying expectations and the amount of parental agency that accompanied them highlighted the distinction between two kinds of parental support for mathematics learning—*rhetorical support,* which was consistent with mere verbalizations of its importance and *substantive, concrete support,* which was also backed up by a more active role in assuring their children's access to mathematics. Rhetorical support exemplifies the fact that:

> Many parents simply don't know how to help their children become high-achievers. The problem is not merely that they fail to emphasize academic achievement, but that they operate on the basis of inappropriate assumptions about when they should intervene, about how they should balance the relative influence of home and school, and about what the most effective socialization techniques are. (Stevenson & Stigler, 1992, p. 93)

This type of support was demonstrated by Harold and Tina, both of whom had little success in mathematics, placed little value on mathematics knowledge, and took no active role in promoting it to their children.

In contrast, both Wendy and Sarah were able to offer substantive support for their children's mathematics learning. Their recent short-term success in mathematics had given them some indications of its utility and importance and caused them to actively insure that their children would gain access to higher-level mathematics.

This positive agency was necessary because all of the participants expressed some resentment about differential treatment, racism, and discrimination in their own lives as well as those of their children. For example, three of the four parents in this chapter developed oppositional relationships with school officials and teachers. There was a strong belief among these parents that the differential treatment experienced by their children from teachers was racially motivated. Sarah, Tina, and Wendy each held the belief that White teachers believed that African-American children were not capable of learning mathematics. They also believed that African-American children did not have advocates in the schools and that teachers were more prone to look out for Asian-American and European-American children.

Given the natures of these community forces and community beliefs about mathematics, one might ask: How do these forces and beliefs play out in the school context to affect interactions among African-American students and their teachers? In chapter 3, I return to the students and teachers at Hillside to address this and other questions.

3

"When Am I Ever Going to Use This?:"

School-Level Factors and Mathematics Socialization Among African-American Students

There is no disputing the fact that schools are complex settings. My stay at Hillside Junior High provided ample evidence and helped me gain a greater appreciation for this fact. Yet, judgments about schools are often reduced to one of two simple conclusions: either a school "works" or it does not. Typically, these judgments are made by focusing on outcome-based measures such at test scores or on descriptive variables such as where the school is located, who the students are, or the level of parental involvement the school receives.

When a school is characterized by many of the conditions that we consider as likely to contribute to problematic achievement and persistence outcomes, we are seldom surprised when these results do occur. But few schools or teachers deliberately set out to shortchange their students. One would suspect that most schools develop mission statements, adopt long-range goals and, for the most part, work toward achieving their stated objectives. In addition, teachers who work in these schools develop their own goals and expectations for their students. Knowing that a school has struggled in its efforts to be successful is not as informative as knowing why. Knowing that students in these schools achieve below their potential or suffer from low motivation is not as informative as knowing why they respond to in-school practices in the ways that they do or why school conditions are such that they contribute to problematic outcomes in achievement and persistence.

In this chapter, I characterize several important school-level factors that affected the conditions for mathematics learning and teaching at Hillside Junior High and that were important considerations in mathematics socialization among its students. Those factors were listed in the third level of the framework introduced in chapter 1. That third level is reproduced below in Table 3.1.

TABLE 3.1
Third Level of Multilevel Framework

School-Level Factors

- Institutional agency and school-based support systems
- Teachers' curricular goals and content decisions
- Teachers' beliefs about student abilities and motivation
- Teachers' beliefs about parents and communities
- Student culture and achievement norms
- Classroom negotiation of mathematical and social norms

Other researchers (e.g., Hale-Benson, 1994; Ladson-Billings, 1994) have focused on documenting culturally relevant or appropriate pedagogy and classroom practices among African-American students and their teachers by selecting teachers and classroom sites where this kind of effective teaching was known to exist. I identified several aspects of this kind of teaching at Hillside, but even their presence was, at times, not enough to overcome other factors—including certain community-level forces—that proved to be obstacles for both teachers and students.

My discussion shows that Hillside Junior High fits the profile of many schools plagued by low student achievement and motivation. But I would not say that Hillside was a school that "didn't work." The situation was more complex than that because there were also conditions that were conducive to effective learning and teaching. These positive forces explain why failure did not always occur and why not all of the students were unmotivated.

My goal in this chapter is not to offer a prescription for what counts as effective teaching or student engagement. Neither is it to say what teachers and students should have done to make mathematics teaching and learning at Hillside more meaningful and effective. What I do offer is a description of what teachers and students actually did on a frequent basis and a partial explanation of why. I also discuss the difficulties encountered when attempts were made to implement novel, reform-oriented mathematics curricula in mathematics classrooms at Hillside and how both internal and external forces made these efforts extraordinarily difficult.

SOCIAL CONTEXT OF HILLSIDE JUNIOR HIGH

Hillside Junior High School is located on the east side of Oakland, California. During the year of my study, the school served approximately 600 students in grades 7 through 9. About 95% of the students were African-American. The remainder of students were White, Asian, Hispanic, and Arab American. During the 1993–1994 school year, 3% of the students were identified as Limited English Proficient. School and district data show that 16% of Hillside students qualified for free or reduced-fee lunch programs and 20% of the students qualified for Aid to Families with Dependent Children. Among sixteen junior high schools in the city, Hillside had the fourth highest SES ranking, ranking behind only three schools that served more middle-class and affluent students. The physical environment at the school, inside and out, can best be described as old and in need of repair. Many of the school's 22 classrooms had suffered the effects of aging, student abuse and neglect.

Achievement Profile

The Oakland Unified School District has been plagued by underachievement for most of its African-American students and, for years, has been criticized by parents, students, and community activists. For example, a 1996 report found that the average grade-point-average of African-Americans district-wide was 1.7.

Like many schools in the district, Hillside experienced its share of problems. A majority of the students were achieving below their potential and there were ongoing problems with discipline and motivation. California Test of Basic Skills (CTBS) percentiles in reading, language, and mathematics for Spring 1993 and 1994, respectively, are given in Table 3.2.

TABLE 3.2
Hillside CTBS Scores, 1993–1994

Grade	Reading	Language	Mathematics
7	26/17	26/16	26/18
8	34/16	22/18	26/14
9	23/34	27/27	20/28

Note: The first and second numbers under each subject represent the percentiles for 1993 and 1994 respectively. For example, 26/17 means that seventh graders scored at the 26th percentile in reading in 1993 and at the 17th percentile in 1994.

These underachievement trends also showed up on quarterly grade assignments. During one marking period, for example, the total number of students throughout the school receiving at least a 2.0 grade-point-average was 216 (approximately 38%) with only 75 of these students maintaining grade-point-averages of 3.0 or higher (approximately 13%). During that same marking period, only 26 seventh-grade students maintained grade-point-averages of at least 3.0 and only 11 maintained grade point averages of at least 3.5. Only one of those seventh-grade students received all As.

Institutional Support Services

The administrative and teacher teams at Hillside consisted of a principal, 2 assistant principals, 2 counselors, 35 regular instruction teachers (most of whom were African-American), 3 special education teachers, 2 resource teachers, a librarian, and a school psychologist.

During the 1993–1994 school year, approximately thirty in-school support services were in place at Hillside, including the Algebra Project. In addition, the school was in the process of implementing the Comer Plan (Comer, 1980) as part of a Superintendent's 5-year restructuring plan that had begun in 1991–1992. The rationale behind selection of the Comer Plan was that it addressed many of the academic, social, and mental health needs of the students and parents served by Hillside. Teachers especially wanted to implement aspects of the model that brought parents into closer contact with the school and also with their children's learning.

Community Supports

In-school efforts at Hillside were supplemented by several community-based programs. One resource that was of particular importance to mathematics socialization at Hillside was a church-based math and science tutorial that serves school children in East Oakland. The program was linked directly to Hillside through a liaison who coordinated the identification of students who were interested in the program. The program was initiated partly to address achievement and persistence issues in mathematics and science among local students and had been in existence for several years. Included in the program were an after-school tutorial and a number of activities designed to expose students to math and science careers and role models. The existence of this program was an indication that some parents and community members recognized the importance of mathematics learning for their children and had acted on that understanding.

Math Teachers

At the time of the study, Hillside had four mathematics teachers. I maintained frequent contact with three of these teachers: Mrs. Allgood who was the department chair, Mr. Brown, and Mr. Olander. Throughout the school, the math teachers were widely acknowledged and respected for their leadership roles. They seemed to represent a close cohort. They were all very involved in school-change procedures, attended numerous conferences, and served on several school committees. They shared similar views and philosophies on teaching, student abilities and motivation, parents, and reforms needed in their school. The fourth mathematics position at Hillside was held by a string of long-term and short-term substitutes. This happened because of problems with the teaching credential of the full-time instructor who had been assigned to this position. He began the year at Hillside but had to leave until these problems were cleared up.

Observation Contexts

I began informal classroom observations at Hillside in the spring of 1993 by spending several days per week in Mr. Olander's seventh-grade sections. I continued to interact with the teachers during the summer of 1993. They met for several hours to plan for the upcoming year and discuss the challenges they faced. These summer meetings were held on a voluntary basis and were held in addition to other staff meetings.

Over the course of the 1993–1994 school year, I spent the majority of my time in three seventh-grade math classes taught by Mrs. Allgood. I observed Mr. Brown and Mr. Olander on a less frequent, informal basis.

Mrs. Allgood taught in a large, square room that was, despite its age, neatly decorated. Desks were usually arranged in long rows of seven or eight unless students were required to work in groups. There was a computer workstation in one corner of the room and enough room for students to write out their work. Mrs. Allgood had a desk and workspace in one corner of the front of the room, but she rarely sat there because she was always making her way around the room to check on students' work.

The size of Mrs. Allgood's classes ranged from 20 to 32 students and, for the most part, each class engaged in the same activities and lessons based on the same teaching style and methods. On most occasions, she introduced activities using an overhead projector at the front of the room and then had students work in groups of three or four on the given activities. Mrs. Allgood maintained the same standards of conduct and behavior throughout all of her classes, and she proceeded with her lessons and plans somewhat independently of the different atmospheres of these classes.

During the first semester, I spent time in her morning session classes—a first period class, a third-period class, and a fourth-period class. The first-period class was the smallest and overwhelmingly female. The class achievement level was such that most students could be characterized as average to slightly above average students. The third-period class was the largest, to the point of being overcrowded—but it was by far the most efficient and contained many good students. The fourth-period class, more than the others, reflected the overall makeup of the rest of the school in terms of attitudes, dispositions, and achievement. There was a small subset of talented, academically oriented students, together with a larger group of students who, based on their actions, did not appear to be interested in classroom activities and who drifted in and out in terms of attention and participation. In the second semester, I frequented the third- and fourth-period classes but focused my observations on the fourth-period class.

During my classroom observations, I split my time between notetaking and in-class tutoring. The complete set of my daily notes served as a chronicle of evolving classroom practices and norms, teacher beliefs and practices, and student beliefs and practices.

Outside of class, I attended assemblies, walked the halls, and spent time in the cafeteria and main office. I also attended evening events at the school such as award ceremonies and talent shows.

Heading into the beginning of the 1993–1994 school year, I was able to see that with all the planning and immediate and pending changes—including implementation of the Comer Model and the Algebra Project curriculum—the teachers and administrators at Hillside had many reasons to be optimistic.

HIGH HOPES AND EXPECTATIONS AT HILLSIDE

If the mathematics teachers at Hillside had had their way, mathematics learning at Hillside would have proceeded somewhat as follows: Upon entering seventh grade all students would enter the Algebra Project curriculum. On any given day, classroom activity would be characterized by highly engaged students working in small groups. They would write about mathematics, communicate their mathematical ideas verbally, and develop various representations of their mathematical experiences. Students would be exposed to such concepts as equivalence, signed numbers and signed number arithmetic, and variables. Teachers would act as facilitators and coaches in students' learning. Student discipline would not be an issue. As students learned more about the connections between their everyday lives and formal mathematics, they would begin to see mathematics in a different light and also gain a greater appreciation for its instrumental importance. Students would also see themselves differently and come to realize that they could participate in various mathematics contexts. By the end of the seventh grade, students would advance into algebra and begin their journey into high-track mathematics.

This was the vision that teachers hoped for in mathematics classrooms at Hillside. To their credit, the mathematics teachers worked very hard to realize this vision, and there were days when their well-made plans proceeded accorded to expectations. My observation notes from Mrs. Allgood's classrooms showed that on these days, students were highly engaged and she was able to carry out her intended plans. I can recall seventh-grade lessons that involved game-like situations such as using dominoes to study number patterns, using the Chinese calendar to study modular equivalence, and having students collect personal data from each other and compile statistics. These activities did build on students' experiences and piqued their interest. On these days, a majority of students appeared to work effectively in their groups and demonstrated high levels of creativity in transforming their everyday experiences into formal mathematical concepts.

Despite these occasional successes, there were many more days that were not like this. Several complicating factors—having to do with teacher goals and expectations, curricular change, student culture and achievement norms, and the impact of community forces—brought about a different, more complex reality. Far too often, mathematics learning and teaching in some classrooms at Hillside did not go as planned. For example, about 3 weeks into the school year, my abbreviated notes included the following comments about one of Mrs. Allgood's seventh-grade classes:

October 20, 1993
Fourth Period   Number of Students: 20

Main Activities: Review of homework
                                  Worksheet on divisibility rules

Mrs. Allgood briefly reviewed the divisibility rules applicable to the activity as students looked on and listened. During her questioning of students, only one or two responded. Others remained silent and refused to raise their hands. Many of the students looked preoccupied and appeared reluctant to make themselves stand out in public. When Mrs. Allgood turned the activity over to the students, things began on a positive note. However, many of the students are only putting in the minimal effort and are easily distracted by others. Many of the students are complaining that the activity is "boring" and "stupid." . . . As I walked around to monitor some of the students, many of them were acting up and becoming disruptive. When I work with them individually, they make an effort to understand. But when left alone, and they have difficulty figuring out the activity, they get loud again. It seems that the students making the most noise are the ones who are the farthest behind or have no idea what's going on . . . The need for discipline in this class is higher than the others. . . . I get the feeling from student comments and their behavior that math and doing well are not high on their priorities. Many don't appear to persist at their work or seek to develop more than a passing understanding. . . . It seems that many students are unmotivated and become easily distracted. This definitely is interfering with their ability to get their work done.

Through the middle of the year, this kind of commentary showed up in my field notes. The nature of the interactions between Mrs. Allgood and her students had not changed to any great degree and, as the year progressed, it was becoming more and more difficult to get some of the students to buy into the mathematical and social demands that she and the Algebra Project curriculum made on them:

March 2, 1994
Fourth Period   Number of students: 19

Today students came in promptly at 11:25. They were somewhat rowdy. Mrs. Allgood began class by imploring them to get their materials from the back of the room. Most of the students were talkative but appeared to obey her commands. She next gave them time to complete some problems from the previous day's worksheet. Several students had lost their worksheets and had to sit there and do nothing. Others had no pencil or kept talking and not working. Some students are trying to work but others are very distracting. One of these students asked to be moved from her group because of the distractions from other students. Mrs. Allgood commented that if all of the students did not quiet down, they would be sent to the office. After 15 minutes or so, she collected the worksheets and began going through the questions. Students were somewhat attentive. One of the [high achieving] students [Jasmine[3]] was visibly frustrated and commented that the material was too easy. As students continued to talk, Mrs. Allgood seemed determined to go on for the few that seemed interested. . . . She then gave them the next activity. As I made my way around the room, not many of the students asked for help because many were talking and some had misinterpreted the instructions for the activity. . . . Class ended with very few of the students having completed the activity even though it was relatively easy.

By the end of the year, not much had changed in the fourth-period classroom. Mrs. Allgood and her students were still engaged in a back-and-forth jostling and negotiation of mathematical and social norms. Although not all of the students in this class had difficulty with the adjustments and demands on their behaviors, many did, and by year's end Mrs. Allgood had grown increasingly discontented. The comments that follow show how little things had progressed:

May 2, 1994
Fourth Period   Number of students: 21

Main Activities: Warm-up on fractions
                                 Concept of *opposite*

Students came in as usual at 11:25. Mrs. Allgood instructed them to get their materials from the back of the room. When they returned to their seats, she gave them a warm-up worksheet on adding fractions with common denominator. Some of the students did not

---

[3] A profile of Jasmine appears in Chapter 4.

have pencils. . . . After 15 minutes, she collected their worksheets and went over the answers. At that time, students became more loud and talkative but quieted somewhat as she put more and more of the answers on the overhead. . . . After reviewing the worksheet, she had students begin working on their curriculum project materials. She quickly explained the activity and students began working. Things started out fairly quiet but soon the noise level and commotion increased. She then kicked two students out of class because of their excessive talking. During the next few minutes, students became less and less attentive and the activity seemed to completely break down for some of them. It is becoming more and more difficult for Mrs. Allgood to explain the activity to students and for students to understand what they are supposed to do. Attention is waning among many of the students but some do continue to work and try to get something done. The atmosphere can get very distracting but Mrs. Allgood continues on and tries to explain for these students. . . . It seems like too much time is being spent on trying to get students' attention and getting them to volunteer for the activities and participate. At this point in the year, some of them have made no progress and they continue to make comments about how boring the class is. It is clear that many of the students are disinterested and are just going through the motions.

Readers should keep in mind that these notes, though they provide some indication of what daily life could be like at Hillside, represent only snapshots of reality. They capture only the essence of what I saw on a typical day. Moreover, although these notes capture a year's experience, this represents only a small time period in the mathematics socializations of students—a process that started long before I arrived and continued to evolve long after I left. Yet, there is much that can be learned in a year's time and I do feel that after a few months, I became more than a casual observer. Although my observation notes provide some indication, they cannot reflect the complexity of events that unfolded at Hillside or the depth of my daily reactions to these events. There were days when my experiences left me full of joy and enthusiasm, but there were many more days when I left with feelings of sadness and confusion.

Moreover, because of my own ideas about what constitutes good teaching, good students, and meaningful teacher-student interactions, I found that I had to exercise restraint in formulating premature explanations of what I was observing. Nevertheless, the interpretive lens that I used to make sense of mathematics learning and teaching at Hillside will probably reflect my many biases. I sympathized with the mathematics teachers because of my own teaching background and the fact that I spent so much time observing them and talking to them; I shared many of their goals for their students. I also sympathized with the students. I could see that some of them worked hard even in the face of potential barriers in and out of school.

On the other hand, I also turned a critical eye toward both teachers and students. I became frustrated with the actions of some students who, for a variety of reasons, refused to take the initiative in their own learning and often criticized or ridiculed other students for wanting to do so. These students would forget to do their homework, come to class without pencil or paper, talk back to the teacher, cause disruptions for other students, and express beliefs that implied mathematics was not important or relevant to them. I agreed with one of the high achieving students who suggested that the administration and teachers spent inordinate amounts of time attending to the disruptions caused by some students but comparatively little time developing programs and efforts aimed at reaching students who wanted to learn. These efforts could be found at Hillside but could have been better developed and could have served students more effectively if teachers did not have to expend so much time and resources attending to problems.

The obvious question for me was: What accounted for the discrepancy between the high hopes and expectations for mathematics learning at Hillside and what actually happened on a more regular basis? Despite the bond that I felt with the teachers and the bonds I felt I was building with some students, my role as a mathematics educator compelled me to look for explanations of why mathematics learning and teaching at Hillside unfolded in the way that it did and to ask questions such as: What were the backgrounds of the teachers charged with students' mathematics socializations? Why did these teachers adopt a goal of having all students complete algebra before leaving Hillside? Why was the Algebra Project curriculum met with resistance by students? Why did an alarming number of students make comments like "I hate math" and "When am I ever going to use this?" Why did teachers attribute these student responses and beliefs, as well as widespread underachievement and attitudinal problems, to the types of negative parent and community beliefs about mathematics that I identified in chapter 2?

TEACHERS AS AGENTS OF
MATHEMATICS SOCIALIZATION

Because mathematics teachers are primary agents of mathematics socialization within the school context—peers being another—I attempted to gain as much information as possible about each of the three math teachers at Hillside.

Much of the data presented about teachers in this chapter comes from interviews but my day-to-day observations were an effective way to determine the level of agreement between the teachers' stated beliefs and their actual classroom practices. I interviewed each teacher separately at the school site. Questions dealt with the following issues: personal backgrounds and educational experiences, their teaching experiences at Hillside, their beliefs about their students' mathematical abilities and motivation to learn mathematics, their beliefs about their students' parents and communities, and their choices of mathematics content and curricular practices. Each interview lasted approximately 1 hour and 30 minutes and was conducted after school.

In their roles as agents of mathematics socialization, math teachers at Hillside faced a number of in-school demands on their teaching, including major curriculum changes, low test scores, low student motivation, and the need to adhere to district and state curriculum standards. As the teachers attempted to meet these demands, they drew on a variety of personal and professional resources and sent a number of mixed messages about mathematics learning and mathematics knowledge to their students.

In the paragraphs that follow, I offer brief snapshots into the personal backgrounds of the teachers—discussing aspects of their own lives and educational experiences. These snapshots also help explain the teachers' beliefs and practices.

Mr. Brown

Mr. Brown is a native of Africa and completed most of his formal education in the country of Sierra Leone. After attending college, where he studied mathematics and statistics, he immigrated to the United States for graduate studies and completed a Ph.D. in statistical demography. As of the fall semester of 1993, he had been teaching in the Oakland Public Schools for approximately 6 years. He had been at Hillside for 5 of those years. During the year of the study, he taught algebra. In addition to his middle school duties, he is also a part-time instructor at a community college.

Mr. Brown was highly involved in school-reform issues and assumed a visible leadership role in school matters. He interacted well with his students but was known as a strict disciplinarian. During his interview comments, Mr. Brown attributed many of his beliefs and attitudes about schooling and the value of education to his own upbringing and the values of his parents and community. He stated that he was struck by the differences between his own educational experiences and those of the students he had come to know at Hillside. This contrast and comparison of his personal experiences with his teaching experiences at Hillside is evident throughout his comments and seemed to account for many of his decisions in the classrooms and his attitudes and beliefs about his students and their parents. These early experiences also contributed to his overall teaching philosophy:

DM: First, let's start out with some background in terms of yourself. Where were you born, where did you grow up, and where did you go to school?

Mr. B: Well, I'm from Sierra Leone, a small West African country on the west coast of Africa with a population that is roughly about 4 million. The educational system is British. Completely different from the American system. . . . I have experienced the two systems of education so I can look at things from the other side and also look at things from this side. . . How to modify whatever I do for the best interests of the students.

DM: Let's say up until college, what was going to school like for you or what kind of memories do you have of when you were going to school?

Mr. B: I mean you *wanted* to go to school. Because the parents are involved. . . . My parents never went to school. They're not educated. It's not like here where at least the parents went to school. [My parents] didn't go to school but they know that's the only way out. That's the only way out in our system. You have to have an education and you have to take it serious.

Mr. Olander

Mr. Olander grew up in Nigeria. He came to the United States in 1986 and began working as a substitute teacher shortly thereafter. He had been at Hillside for 5 years by the time of the study. He earned undergraduate degrees in physics and computer science and developed an interest in education while pursuing graduate studies in computer science. Of the three math teachers at Hillside, Mr. Olander seemed to be the most popular among students.

During the year in which the study took place, Mr. Olander taught algebra and geometry. In preparation for the formal study, I spent a semester in one of Mr. Olander's seventh-grade sections during the Spring of 1993. I also spent the next summer informally observing Mr. Olander in planning sessions and interacted with him on several occasions throughout the school year. He assisted me in the study by providing the names of high achieving students enrolled in his geometry course and giving me student responses to a survey about mathematics.

Like Mr. Brown, Mr. Olander talked at great length about his own education and how it differed from what he had experienced and observed among his students. His own early experiences in mathematics and science, in particular, had left a lasting impression on him. His early life and educational experiences also appeared to constitute the basis for his beliefs about ideal ways of knowing and behaving, especially his belief in maintaining high standards and personal accountability for his students. In the comments that follow, he recalled the adjustment that he had made when he first began teaching students at Hillside:

DM: You mentioned that you started here about 4 or 5 years ago? You said it was kind of an initial shock? Different than the way that you went to school? What was it like when you were going to school? What were your experiences?

Mr. O: Well, I've shared this a lot with my students, too. Schooling where I came from is different in the sense that here I notice that the kids take education for granted. . . . But where I come from, parents have to pay for their kids to go to school . . . . So, when you go to school you have to know why you're there. The teachers don't have to tell you why you're there. . . .There's an immense pressure on every parent to train their kids. So, I don't care how poor a parent is, they will look for a way to get money. . . . Their last penny will be spent for their kid to be in school. You have to do it. If you don't, society will look down on you. So, all those types of pressures and things make school what it is. Kids wanting to succeed. . . . You don't have that here. . . . I remember the first time I came here, I turned in my first report card grades. I had parents almost mobbing me because I gave some grades that they didn't like. I had parents who were telling me to change the grade. That really was a shock to me because I could not imagine coming home with a report card and my father going back to attack my teacher. If I came back with a wrong report card, I don't care what my story is, my father would get on me and not the teacher. That was one of my first shocks when I came here—to understand that the system is different. . . . To me, it was an eye opener and I just knew that something was different, something was wrong.

Mrs. Allgood

Mrs. Allgood was the most experienced of the math teachers at Hillside, having taught there for over 15 years. She grew up in Louisiana and attended college there as well. Her major was biological sciences with a math minor. She indicated that she had originally wanted to teach biology, but when she came to California, there were several opportunities available in math teaching and she chose one of those. Before coming to California, she taught in several midwestern states. During the year of the study, she taught mostly seventh-grade sections, using the Algebra Project curriculum, and one or two sections of algebra. Mrs. Allgood appeared to have a reasonable mastery of the material that she taught, although her knowledge of the subject matter was not as strong as Mr. Brown's or Mr. Olander's.

Mrs. Allgood was regarded as a strict disciplinarian by her students and conducted her classes by adhering to both the rules of the school and the rules that she maintained specifically for her classrooms. During her teaching, she usually had a serious demeanor, was very organized, and did not tolerate disruptive student behavior. She dealt with disruptions swiftly and abruptly, often sending students out of class or scolding them for not bringing materials or for not paying attention. Like Mr. Brown and Mr. Olander, her personal experiences strongly influenced her beliefs about the role and importance of education:

DM: Did you go to public or private schools?

Mrs. A: Public schools.

DM: And what was going to school like for you back then? What do you remember about it?

Mrs. A: Oh, I remember you *went* to school. You went to school and school was your job. Yes, it was your job to learn as much as you possibly could and to do as much as you possibly could to advance yourself. Although you had other duties than school, you still had school as your number one priority. . . . Because that's the way my parents and

grandparents and everybody believed. That school was
important and they were involved in the school and in the
community as well.

Although she expressed high levels of concern and frustration
about student behaviors and lamented that too few of the students
cared about school or mathematics, Mrs. Allgood, like Mr. Brown and
Mr. Olander, balanced these beliefs by maintaining a certain level of
confidence in her students' abilities. She also demonstrated this in her
classroom teaching by continuing to demand that students improve
their skills and behaviors and by holding them accountable for their
actions:

DM: So, during that time what's been your philosophy on
        teaching?

Mrs. A: I think all students are capable of learning maybe not at the
         same rate but they can all learn and they don't all learn the
         same way. But they can do something. That's my
         philosophy—they can do something. If they can't write
         words then I think they should be able to draw symbols. If
         they can't do computation on a higher scale, at least the
         basics. Knowing their facts, whether it's addition,
         subtraction, multiplication or division and be able to
         recognize these things and apply them to some new
         situations. And I'm not finding that happening. We seem
         to be going backwards.

                    ....

DM: What do you think are the biggest strengths and biggest
        weaknesses for most of the students in terms of their math
        backgrounds?

Mrs. A: Their biggest strength is that, I guess, they're capable of
         learning. Their weakest area is the fact that they don't apply
         what they already know. If you dig into a problem with
         them, then they are subject to follow along with you and
         give you responses, which lets you know that they have
         some understanding of what the problem is about. But if
         you leave them to do it on their own and not guide them in
         some way, they will sit there and say "I can't do this. I don't
         know how to do this," and not put anything at all on their
         paper.

When I asked her what she believed her students thought about
her teaching philosophy and the expectations that she had for them,

Mrs. Allgood indicated that there was a striking difference in perspective between what she thought was best for students and what they thought. This difference was partly responsible for some of the difficulties that occurred between students and the math teachers at Hillside:

Mrs. A: I don't think they think that I really care about them. Because I tend to think that they should be responsible for what they need in the classroom as far as material and mental responsibility. I care about them to the point that I'm willing to help them in any way that they can't help themselves. I don't think I'm getting that across to them and so it comes on like, "Mrs. Allgood doesn't care if I have a headache, or if I can't do my work today, or if I need a pencil, or if I don't get this answer. She should give me a pencil or she should give me the answer." What they consider as caring, I consider as crippling because I know that no one, once they leave school, will be giving them legitimate answers to questions that they will find as problems, be it in math or some other area. They will have to start thinking for themselves. . . . So, I guess that's a weakness that I have in trying to show them that I really care by expecting them to be responsible for what they do and how they do it.

Teacher Goals.

After interviewing and observing each of the teachers, I was able to identify five general goals that appeared to guide their in-class behaviors and interactions with their students. These goals were consistent with the vision set forth in the early part of this chapter:

- Raising the achievement and motivation levels of students.

- Changing student beliefs about the nature of mathematical practice.

- Changing student beliefs about the instrumental importance of mathematics.

- Adhering to standards and beginning to implement reform-oriented activities.

- Increasing parental involvement and awareness of students' in class activities.

Achieving these goals proved to be especially difficult. But the mathematics teachers were unwavering in their attempts and were determined to overcome the problems at their school:

> Mrs. A: I want all [students] to do especially well on the standardized tests that are coming up. I do believe that the stigma that our school has gotten as a result of low test scores, low GPA, that it can be turned around. That's what the math people are still trying to work toward. That's our number one priority—trying to turn around low test scores, low GPAs and also to make sure that the students leave one grade knowing what they need to know in order to be successful in the next grade level.

CURRICULAR CHANGE AS A CONTEXT FOR MATHEMATICS SOCIALIZATION

In many ways, the organization of the mathematics curriculum at Hillside set it apart from other middle schools in the district. The mathematics teachers at Hillside were concerned that few African-American students were going on to additional mathematics beyond prealgebra and had chosen the Algebra Project curriculum to help address this concern. From the teachers' point of view, it helped them provide students with an early lead into algebra. The following comment by Mr. Olander succinctly summarized the rationale behind the teachers' choice of curriculum:

> Mr. O: Well, the broad goal here is to make sure that by the time the students leave our school, they have taken algebra.

This goal was almost assured, given that after completing the Algebra Project curriculum project in their seventh grade year, students were assigned to Algebra I, a year long, fast-track introduction to elementary algebra, or to Algebra A. Algebra A was the first half of the Algebra I course but was taught over two semesters. Students who completed Algebra I in eighth grade were then assigned to geometry in ninth grade. Students who completed Algebra A in eighth grade were then assigned to Algebra B in the ninth grade (Algebra B was the second half of the regular Algebra I course). Unless students failed at some point, they were guaranteed to have taken algebra by the end of their ninth-grade year and could then go on to take college preparatory mathematics if they chose to do so and if their high school offered advanced courses.

There was a concerted decision among the mathematics teachers and administrative team at Hillside to organize the mathematics curriculum in this way. Besides serving as a context to change the nature of students' mathematics socializations, the change to the Algebra Project curriculum fit in very well with the school's overall restructuring efforts. Also, because the math teachers were aware of state and national reform efforts, they were concerned about selecting activities and curriculum units that they believed confirmed to the spirit of these reforms. The Algebra Project allowed for and stressed many of the practices found not only in district and state standards (California State Department of Education, 1992; Oakland California Unified School District, 1993) but also in the National Council of Teachers of Mathematics (NCTM) *Standards* (NCTM, 1989). During planning meetings held during the summer of 1993, the mathematics teachers carefully reviewed the activities they had chosen and their sequencing to insure that their goals would be achieved. Mr. Brown and Mr. Olander characterized their curricular goals in the following way:

Mr. B: Basically, all our goals that we set were really all in line with either the [district's] Core Curriculum or the State *Framework*. That's what we are heading towards. The Algebra Project is different from all other schools. We are the only one that does this kind of program.

....

Mr. O: Well, one of our biggest goals this year is to see if we can begin to implement the replacement units that are mandated by the State. . . . One of my biggest challenges this year is to begin to train my kids to express their ideas more, to communicate their ideas more. . . . The *Framework* says that mathematical power is being able to communicate ideas. A lot of kids have these ideas but they cannot express it, write it out, even if it's by drawing, by whatever.

DM: How much of that was influenced by the core curriculum and NCTM *Standards*?

Mr. O: Almost everything there is influenced by that. That is the shift, we are laying more and more emphasis on making sure that we are guided by the [California] Math *Framework* and the NCTM *Standards*.

Although the math teachers made several references to their efforts to implement practices found in the NCTM Standards and California Mathematics *Framework* (California State Department of Education, 1992) they also expressed some skepticism about those documents. At one point in her interview, Mrs. Allgood stated that many of the practices stressed in these curriculum guidelines were "the same kinds of things we have been doing for years. They've just given it a new name and that doesn't make it any more effective than it has been." Mr. Olander, also expressed concerns about assessment practices and how these practices are applied to African-American students:

Mr. O: One thing I found out is that the tests that we give our kids are not made from the point of view of the backgrounds of our students. Not even of our own teachers. Most of the things that have been happening in California, I found out that many of them are organized, written, designed by teachers from Southern California, from Fresno, from Bakersfield, from all these suburb schools and things. So when you come to look at it really, most of the questions are not asked from the point of view of our kids. So, I believe that if we want our kids to perform very well these days, we have to begin to teach our kids how to take tests. The test does not necessarily measure what the kids know. Sometimes a lot of the problem is that these kids do not understand the purpose of the test. They do not have these test-taking strategies. I've seen kids here take a test. . . . Some of them just get the test paper and just bubble it in all the way down. I've had a kid in my class take a test that was supposed to last for 45 minutes, in 5 minutes. I went back and looked at the booklet and I know that I cannot do that test in 20 minutes. How could you finish in 5 minutes? So, part of the thing is we have to train our kids on how to take tests. Then we have to begin to include teachers from these Black schools to attend those workshops, those conferences where these tests are designed. There are people who are already in these things year in, year out. They know what is wanted. They give it to their students. Their students perform very well in the test. I don't know what is wanted on those tests. I did not contribute to the questions. Therefore, a lot of times, it trickles down to our kids not being able to answer.

I highlight these comments because questions of "Whose standards?" and "For whom?" have been raised in discussions of the fates of African-American students in the context of the current mathematics education reform movement (Secada, 1992; Stiff, 1990; Tate, 1994, 1995). The difficulties Mrs. Allgood's students experienced with the reform-oriented practices they encountered highlighted a serious mismatch between students and teachers in their beliefs about what counts as mathematics. The fact that students did not buy into many of their reform-oriented classroom activities or think of them as "real math" had serious consequences for their achievement. Whether or not this "mismatch" is or will become widespread among African-American students and their teachers in other schools is an interesting question that needs further study.

Effects of Curricular Change on Student Beliefs About Mathematics

One outcome that teachers had hoped to achieve as a result of their curricular reorganization was to alter their students' beliefs about mathematics and prevent days like those described earlier in this chapter from occurring on a regular basis. In particular, they wanted to change their students' beliefs about the ways in which one engages in mathematical practices. The Algebra Project activities, in particular, required students to engage in several new ways of doing mathematics—discussion, drawing, and cooperative learning. On several occasions, teachers expressed reservations about whether their goal of getting students to buy into these practices was being achieved. Also, these activities appeared to have little effect on changing students' beliefs about mathematics or its importance; many of the students characterized their classroom activities as "boring" and expressed a desire to work in traditional math books. In displaying their resistance, some students consistently engaged in one or more of the following problematic behaviors: coming to class late and unprepared with pencil or paper, turning in incomplete work or failing to turn in their assigned work, missing several days of class, and disrupting classroom activities by interfering with other students. Mrs. Allgood explained:

DM: You mentioned the Algebra Project. What's your feeling about it so far?

Mrs. A: I think [the Algebra Project] has been a success with some students but not all. I really feel that our seventh graders are beginning to think that they are too sophisticated for the types of activities that we do. And by sophisticated I mean that they don't see discussion of mathematics being

mathematics. The Algebra Project requires a lot of
discussion. It's a lot of interacting and it may not be all
numbers. They tend to think that if they are not doing
number activities, then it's not math. So, for some, as I said,
they like it. For many more, they don't like it. They're not
used to writing in math more than filling in a blank with
one word or one number. So it makes quite a difference in
how they feel about the algebra course. You've probably
heard them say "This isn't math. I don't like this." . . . But
at this point, it's hard for them to recognize what a picture
has to do with math or what a sentence has to do with math
or what a discussion has to do with math.

Although Mr. Brown did not teach from the Algebra Project
curriculum during the year of the study, he had taught it the previous
year and was able to expand on Mrs. Allgood's explanation:

DM: Do you think [students realize why they are participating
        in your special math curriculum project] or why they have
        to do some of those things like discussion and writing and
        drawing?

Mr. B: Well, they were told why. But again, all along for the past 6
        years these kids have been doing something different. All
        of a sudden in seventh grade, you're telling them to do
        things otherwise. . . . So, there is a lot of resistance. It's not
        working here in seventh grade.

DM: Is it the content, or is the way that students are supposed to
        engage in mathematics?

Mr. B: Well, the content is new to the students and it's a completely
        different approach. There's a sudden change in the way the
        students look at mathematics and the way the project looks
        at mathematics. For the students, mathematics means
        adding, subtracting, dividing, and multiplying, and that's
        it. It's not something you sit and talk about. This is not their
        concept of math. It's not something you write about. You
        have to add or subtract and there must be a correct answer.
        Now at this level, we're saying no, no, no. There's no one
        correct answer. That's a very, very difficult task for people
        at this age. They want immediate gratification. There must
        be a correct answer. There shouldn't be two ways.

The fact that many students still preferred their old ways of doing
and learning mathematics and had difficulties adjusting to the
demands of the new curriculum practices was echoed in comments

made by Carl, one of the high-achieving, seventh-grade students whom I interviewed in the study:

DM: Do you like the kind of math you do in class? You have to write a lot, you have to draw pictures, and sometimes you have to discuss stuff out loud. Do you like that way of doing math?

C: Not really. Like I said, I think we should work in the math books more.

DM: Do you know why you're working on the [seventh-grade curriculum project]? Did anybody tell you?

C: [Mrs. Allgood] hasn't really explained.

DM: The Algebra Project work, do you see it as real math?

C: Partly math.

DM: Which part is the math part?

C: Where we do fractions and stuff. Make decimals out of fractions.

DM: What about the writing and the pictures?

C: Doubt it. Because math is basically where you're adding things, and subtraction, and dividing. I don't think that in math you're drawing pictures. That's for art.

Another seventh-grade student, Sheneka, had similar comments about the reform-oriented materials being used in her mathematics classroom:

DM: What about the kind of math you do in math class? Do you like it?

S: Not really. Because I like doing work out of the math book.

DM: In your [Algebra Project curriculum materials] you have to write a lot. Do you like writing in math class?

S: I like doing math. I don't like writing.

DM: You don't see writing as a part of doing math?

S: Um um ... numbers have more to do with math than words.

Another goal for the teachers—also related to their curricular re-organization—was to change students' conceptions about the instrumental importance of mathematics knowledge. My observations of and interactions with the teachers showed that they had very strong beliefs about the instrumentality of mathematics. They also believed that studying mathematics would help their students gain access to opportunities not otherwise available. When asked directly why they wanted their students to learn mathematics and if they thought their students had an interest in learning mathematics, Mrs. Allgood and Mr. Olander responded as follows:

> Mrs. A: I think math is a part of every phase of life. From the time they get up in the morning to the time they go to bed at night. They should be able to apply math to any situation that comes up where mathematics is needed, whether it's their bus schedule, whether it's their money for lunch, whether it's for an activity after school, going to the mall, wherever they love going, they're going to have to have some dealings with math. So that is my real reason, that they should be able to take math, learn math so they will be able to apply it to any situation in life that they might need and not blame somebody else for not having learned something.

> ....

> Mr. O: So, I tell them this all the time . . . that math is going to be . . . a major factor in the 21st century. That if you need a job, the higher the pay depends on how much math you have. If you have don't have math, you're going to sit in the parking lots and open the gates. If you have a lot of math, you will probably will be somewhere up in the office calculating things, using graphs and all that. So, I tell them that just to let them see the usefulness of math.

To get students to develop beliefs similar to theirs, the teachers grounded a portion of students' in-class activities in their everyday experiences. In fact, a large part of the Algebra Project curriculum was based on having the students make connections between a real-world event that they experienced as a group—a trip on a local rail system—and the formal mathematics of algebra. Mrs. Allgood also chose activities such as having students interview parents and community members to find out how they used mathematics in their everyday lives and jobs. She entitled this activity "Math in My Community." Each day over the course of 3 weeks, she had a few students give reports on whom they had interviewed and what they had learned about how these people used math in their jobs or daily lives. Mrs. Allgood was pleased with the students' efforts, and I also observed several students present interesting stories about people who used mathematics in various ways. This activity, although successful for the short term, appeared to have a minimal effect on changing a majority of the students' fundamental beliefs about the utility of mathematics or in getting them to think about mathematics in broader terms beyond the school context. Mrs. Allgood commented that two common questions among students were "When am I ever going to use this?" and "When am I going to need this outside of this classroom?" The fact that students continued to ask these questions long after their community interviews were over raises questions about the messages students may be getting from society and their communities about the role and importance of mathematics in their lives.

In addition to the difficulties students encountered in adjusting to the Algebra Project curriculum, another factor affected the ability of teachers to act effectively in their roles as agents of mathematics socialization: All three teachers commented on the tensions that arose between what they considered content-centered goals and what they saw as student-centered goals. On the one hand, the teachers wanted students to be responsible for learning specific mathematics content and engaging in the practices stressed in the Algebra Project curriculum. On the other hand, they wanted to support their students' emotional needs but in ways that did not handicap students or relieve them from their responsibility of learning as much as they could. For example, when discussing the outcomes he hoped to obtain from his students, Mr. Olander at one point appealed to the need to have students master specific skills:

DM: What would you consider success for [your] students? What is it you're trying to get out of them?

Mr. O: Well, first if there is some specified skill as far as I'm concerned. Once those skills are learned, I would consider that kid successful at that level. If that kid does not learn those skills and grasp the concepts embedded, then that kid will not have been successful. That is my way of measuring. I know that there are some teachers who will not agree with me. There are teachers who feel that if a kid comes to class enough times, just showing up in class, that's enough for that kid to pass. I don't believe that. I believe that if you come to class, you should also be there to learn

something. If you get whatever it is, then I will tell you that
you are succeeding. Anything short of that is not successful.

Mr. Olander continued to elaborate on this content-centered goal
by discussing his preference for remaining true to his standards rather
than compromising them in favor of accommodating students or
letting them pass based on lowered expectations:

> Mr. O: I have always insisted on maintaining a particular standard,
> not falling below a certain level. I always insist on that. . . .
> I would prefer to put in time. I prefer to stay after school. I
> prefer to give up my lunch to help any student who needs
> help rather than bring down my standards just because
> certain students are not doing well. I would rather help
> you to bring that [grade] up than lower the standard to
> accommodate everybody. So that's one key thing that I have
> taken out of all this. I still want to keep a hold on it.

But later in his interview, Mr. Olander revealed the true nature of
the tensions that teachers face in their efforts to simultaneously help
students with their mathematical and emotional development. He told
me a story about his interactions with a student who could not
demonstrate a basic mathematical skill when asked to do so. In
analyzing the student's behavior, Mr. Olander found that an
understanding of the student's mathematical behavior was closely tied
to an understanding of the student's social behavior, including a
tendency for the student to act up in class. Furthermore, from Mr.
Olander's point of view, the roots of this student's behavior may have
stemmed from out-of-school forces that interfered with the students'
ability to focus on learning. These out-of-school factors interfered not
only with the student's learning but also with Mr. Olander's ability to
teach:

> Mr. O: I once found out from one of my students—it was a
> shocking discovery—the student could not multiply two
> 2-digit numbers. That was terrible to me. But then I found
> out that his way of covering up this deficiency [was] by
> acting up in class. There are some students who I believe
> have the capacity to perform very well in math but . . . a lot
> of kids have problems that have nothing to do with school.
> . . . We have lots of problems, combinations of problems,
> that these kids go through. Those are the big things that
> get in the way. . . . There's nothing we can do as a teacher.
> We just pray that each day that comes around, you will get
> at least a larger part of the time for that day [to teach]. . . .

> What I feel, personally, and I do not want to blame anybody for it, but we have had to deal with more behavioral problems in the classroom. If there's any big disappointment that I have teaching is the fact that we are spending an increasing amount of time on discipline rather than on teaching. Behavior problems, disruptions, and all that are taking an increasing amount of time. Something has to be done about it because we are wasting a lot of time, a lot of valuable learning time. . . . When you go through these teacher training programs, you don't spend any time, you don't take any classes that deal with how to deal with student behavior. But then you come into a classroom, you're spending more that half the time on student behavior. It's becoming a major problem.

Because of the tensions that existed between these student-centered and content-centered goals, I observed Mrs. Allgood and her students, for example, consistently engage in back-and-forth resistance and enforcement of both the practices found in the Algebra Project and Mrs. Allgood's own guidelines for student conduct in her classroom. This back and forth often changed the nature of the classroom activities and the focus of instruction. My observation notes from Mrs. Allgood's fourth-period class show how, over the course of a few days, she and her students bounced back and forth between engaged teaching and learning to disengagement:

December 14, 1993
Fourth Period   Number of students: 18

Main Activities: Statistics—mean, median, mode

Students came in and Mrs. Allgood immediately had them get their [curriculum materials]. She told them that she would be checking yesterday's homework, pp. 14–17. She told them to continue their work from yesterday and finish what they had not done. There were three adults in class today and we each helped the students. Just about everyone was doing something or making an attempt to do something, including the table in the back. The room is buzzing with activity. Even [Darryl] is trying and has been asking for help the last couple of days. The class is very active today. Not all the time was spent on math but several students were trying to get something done. . . . The atmosphere in today's class is hard to judge. The students were working and are on–task but some were behind, some finish early, and some start but don't finish their work. Still, with the adult help in the room, students are showing that they can work if they want to. . . . After class, Mrs. Allgood commented that she was pleased with the way the students stayed on–task and said "I think they're getting it. I'm beginning to see the light at the end of the tunnel. I think they're working more because they finally see numbers in their work."

Despite being pleased with her students' earlier behavior, 2 days later things had changed dramatically, and Mrs. Allgood and her students found themselves in different moods:

December 16, 1993
Fourth Period   Number of students: 18

Main Activities: Meaning of equivalence

Mrs. Allgood had to start this class off with a very stern voice. Students came in rowdy and inattentive. She spent several minutes trying to start class and get their attention. She had students turn to p. 18 in their [curriculum materials]. She still had trouble getting their attention and had to kick [Ricky] out of class for being too disruptive. . . . She didn't spend a lot of time on the instructions for the new activity because the students had irked her. By this time, students had quieted down but were still only partly paying attention. She told them to work on pp. 19–21. I made my way around the room to see what students were doing. As it turned out, despite their rowdy behavior, most had managed to complete the previous homework and begin the new material. . . . It was especially surprising to see [Kim, Cindy, Russell] and some others get something done. . . . Several of the students seemed confused by the new words on their assignment like "context" and "equivalence" and only a few managed to make it to p. 21. . . . It seems like some students still have made little sense of what they are doing and continue to make negative comments: [Kim]—"This is boring" [Mark]—"Math is stupid."

STUDENT CULTURE AND THE ROLE OF PEERS IN MATHEMATICS SOCIALIZATION

As I indicated, dramatic changes in the mathematics curriculum led to a great deal of resistance by many students. But some students also allowed other factors—namely, peers—to affect their behaviors and dispositions in their math classrooms. My observations suggest there were two main student groups at Hillside. Both teachers and students alike confirmed that academic achievement and a desire to achieve seemed to be the major factors defining these two groups. The dominant student group and the norms promoted within in it were characterized by underachievement and a host of beliefs and behaviors that appeared to perpetuate low levels of achievement. A much smaller group of students were more successful in their academic efforts. Mr. Olander distinguished these groups as follows:

> Mr. O: There are some students who, success to them means just coming to class, success to them means just passing, with a D minus, anything as long as it's not F. That's success to them. Then you have some students who will not want anything less than an A. . . . Frankly, we can say so much about these kids but a lot of times we tend to ignore the fact that there are some kids, even among these kids, who are great models, they are doing everything you want them to do, they're doing homework, their parents are involved. We have those kids. Sometimes, frankly, I believe that I draw a lot of my strength from all these kids. You know at least there is somebody who wants to learn. Therefore, I have to really give that extra effort. There are some of them that are learning. Learning skills, getting everything that you want them to get. On the other hand, you have the ones that are really at the bottom. They're not learning anything, they're just wasting time.

Students in these two groups, for the most part, did not avoid each other. They interacted on a daily basis and maintained friendships, but there was no doubt that the line was clearly drawn when it came to academics and classroom behavior. Academically successful students were more likely to put forth the effort to meet the mathematical and social demands that were placed on them. But the attitudinal norms and behaviors characterizing the dominant student culture often clashed with those called for in classroom and curricular practices. This led to increased tensions between Mrs. Allgood and some of her students as well as among students themselves. Mrs. Allgood commented about the different roles peers played in influencing student behaviors, particularly for mathematics learning. She explained how most of the high-achieving students appeared to separate their academic and social lives and did not let their friendships interfere with their studies. On the other hand, many of the low-achieving students appeared to be more influenced by their peers and did not display any consistent effort or motivation to do well:

> DM: What about the kids' interest in math? Do you find that math means anything to them?

> Mrs. A: I wish I could say yes but math seems to be everybody's least favorite subject except for people who are teaching it.

> There are some kids, as I said before, who are capable of
> doing the math and who really love the math. But peer
> pressure keeps the students from really succeeding. . . . The
> seventh graders that I have, they tend to not want their
> peers to know that they are capable of doing much better
> work and that they like math for fear that [other] students
> might think [they're] the teacher's pet or [they're] just trying
> to please the teacher. . . . It seems as though if they know an
> answer, they have to look around and if no one else says it
> [they] won't say it either. [They might think] "I know [the
> answer] but I'm not going to say it because they'll think
> I'm a nerd or I'm being a smarty pants." They are more
> influenced by their peers' negative thoughts than positive
> ones.

Mrs. Allgood's comments and perceptions appeared accurate. As
I made my way around to various groups in her classrooms, I could
sense that many students were hesitant to make their knowledge public
if the tone of the class appeared to be hostile—usually because of the
actions of a few students who became openly critical of others. For
me, the implications of these kinds of peer group influences on
students' mathematics socializations are clear. If doing well in
mathematics is given a negative connotation among students, then
the factors contributing to students' mathematics success and failure
are not confined to teacher attitude, biased curriculum, and student
background but are also affected by attitudinal and behavioral norms
that exist among students themselves. To counter these norms, students
must be encouraged and helped to develop strong personal identities
and the kind of individual agency that are able to withstand these
pressures.

COMMUNITY FORCES AND
IN-SCHOOL MATHEMATICS SOCIALIZATION

Mrs. Allgood, Mr. Olander, and Mr. Brown all believed they were doing
as much as they could within the school context to achieve their goals
and help students succeed in mathematics. In this section, I discuss
how teachers cited a lack of parental support as another major factor
affecting their ability to achieve the goals they set for their students.

In the previous chapter, three of the four parents and community
members whom I interviewed characterized teachers in a mostly
negative light and appeared to develop oppositional relationships with
them. It is certainly reasonable to assume that students are aware of
both the positive and strained relationships that parents have with

teachers and that some students bring various elements of these community forces with them when they come to school. It is also reasonable to assume that teachers respond to and interact with their students in ways that demonstrate support for or disapproval of these community forces.

At Hillside, teachers and administrators spent enormous amounts of time trying to implement programs that countered negative aspects of community forces and that brought parents into closer contact with the school. Parents were asked to serve as volunteers in students' classrooms. Very few did. Parents were sent surveys asking them to comment about what they believed happened in their children's school and classrooms and they were asked to make suggestions for improvement. Few parents responded. Teachers and administrators also scheduled several evening events during which parents and their children had the opportunity to meet with teachers and talk about pertinent issues at Hillside. I attended several of these events, including concerts and student honor nights, and observed that the small group of parents who did attend were usually the parents of students who were doing well. Typically, parents of the students who were not doing well only came to school to resolve problematic issues related to their child's behavior, if they came at all.

When asked what roles they wanted parents to assume in their children's education, the math teachers were unanimous in their responses. More than anything else, they expressed a desire for parents to spend time in their children' classrooms, not necessarily to assist teachers but to gain a better understanding of the teacher's job, the activities and practices in which their children engaged, and the difficulties associated with teaching. Mr. Olander and Mrs. Allgood echoed these sentiments with the additional condition that parents "sign a contract" requiring them to visit their child's classroom:

Mr. O: If I had the power to change things, one of the biggest things is that I would make parents sign a contract to come in and spend at least 1 hour a month in the classroom with their kids. . . . That way they will have a feel for what we go through here. They will understand what a school day is like here. . . . I would never have known what school is like if I was not involved here. . . . So, those parents need to come in here and spend one full day and see what it is like. Maybe after that they will know that "Hey, I have to do something about this. I have to try and help my kid." If I had the power, that's just what I would do.

....

Mrs. A: I really would like to have the parent, the child, and the teacher just sit down together at some point at the beginning of the school year and not have just have the teacher making rules about what is expected but the parent also. Let the teacher know "These are my expectations for my child." I'll sign off on it. They sign my expectation, I sign their expectation and then we keep in touch with each other.

I informed the teachers that I had been interviewing parents for my study and I asked them what kinds of questions they would like me to pose to these parents. Again, their responses reflected a very strong belief that parents were unconcerned and uninvolved in students' educations:

Mr. B: The thing I would really want to know is how involved they are in their kid's education. Do they actually take the time to ask Johnny "What did you do in school today? Can I see what you did?" . . . So, really, I want to know why they are not so involved in what the kids are doing. Whether, in fact, they are interested. How often do they actually visit the school? How often do they call the teachers to check on their kids? If we can get 10 to 15 parents every day here, all this nonsense would not be going on around here.

....

Mr. O: I want to know from the parents, "How many times have you visited your child's school on an average month or an average week? How many times did you visit your kid's school on an average month? How much time do you spend with your kid helping your kid with their work or going through your kid's work or discussing what your kid or doing in school or appreciating the things that your kid is doing right? How many times have you talked to the teacher, I mean initiating it, calling the teacher to find out without just being prompted by the report card or some other thing?" Some of the parents may be of the impression that the teachers have to do the miracle. . . . Teachers have their part, parents will have their part. I believe that their part should be taken care of if we are going to see success for our kids.

The math teachers also commented that a major factor differentiating successful students from their less successful peers was the amount of support these students received from their parents:

Mr. B: Perhaps one of the other things is that the few that do well, when you really look at it closely, there's a major parental involvement. When you talk to [successful] kids they tell you "I cannot take a C home." So that tells you that the parents have said "You can't bring a C here. That's not the grade we're looking [for]." . . . You see these kids work towards that. The other kids that don't do well, when you really ask them, most of the time their parents really don't care. . . . Now you look at other kids who are going to get F's, they say "I don't care." So, I don't know whether this is part of the attitude they have. They don't take work seriously because there are no consequences at home.

One of the questions that I raised in chapter 2 concerned the ways in which parents' mathematical experiences affect those of their children. The math teachers at Hillside were also aware of these potential effects and provided their own answers to this question. All three teachers cited parents' own lack of success in mathematics as a major reason that parents did not spend more time in their children's mathematics classrooms or monitor their mathematics achievement more closely. Moreover, the teachers also believed that many students may have interpreted their parents' absence at school as providing both explicit and implicit messages about the importance of mathematics learning and knowledge:

Mr. O: Some of [the students] don't like math and I don't believe that it's because it's something that's intrinsic. I believe that a lot of them, it's probably something that they perceive or have heard somebody say—maybe a mom or dad or somebody say "Hey, [math] is difficult" and they just buy into it. . . . I don't have parents who are pushing me right now to see how their kids are doing in math. . . . See, we are teaching a class where most parents have this fear for math. Some of them have been intimidated by that word *math*. They don't want to get too close to it because of their own personal experiences. Even if you invite them to come and sit in the class, a lot of them don't want to be there because they don't want to answer any questions or show that they cannot answer a question. So, a lot of them prefer not to be around.

DM: Do you think that rubs off on the students at all, or do you think students pick it up, or you're not really sure?

Mr. O: Of course, if parents show interest in their kids' work, the kids will begin to do much more. But if nobody is showing interest then, at some point, [the kids] will just say, "Hey, I don't care.

Mr. B: Most of the parents, really I've talked to them. The first
          thing they tell you is "I was not good in math." So, it's like
          they are also scared even to help the kids because they didn't
          do well in this subject so how they can help the kids do it.
          But it's the interest. You should show the interest. . . .
          Probably, they didn't go up to this level that the kids are
          going, so they're kind of scared to really know what is going
          on.

                            ....

Mrs. A: Well, the few parents that I have reached are concerned.
          However they are not sure what to do if they are having
          problems with their children. . . . Where parents are capable
          of helping their children, they will. Where they're not, I
          guess they tend to make excuses like "I didn't like math
          when I was in school, so I can understand why my child
          probably doesn't."

At one point during the school year, the math teachers had become
so frustrated by underachievement and low motivation among
students that they decided to seek explanations from the students
themselves. They prepared and distributed a survey to students and
conducted whole-class follow-up discussions that centered on the issue
of why students suffered from low motivation. Although the teachers
did not formally analyze the survey responses or the groups'
discussions, they did notice particular patterns of responses among
their students. I was able to confirm these patterns after looking
through several hundred of the surveys and by listening to one of the
group discussions. The teachers and I both noticed that a significant
number of students, high achieving and low achieving alike, shared
the perception that some parents were not concerned about how their
children were doing in school. Mr. Brown and Mrs. Allgood
summarized the motivation for the survey and our common findings:

Mr. B: Well, I think we noticed that even with all these nice
          programs [we have]. . . . You can pour in millions of dollars
          here. If the kids are not motivated to take advantage of what
          you have, then you're wasting your time. So we thought
          perhaps we need to find out why they are not motivated
          . . . . So we took out a survey. . . . [Some of the questions we
          asked were] "Why do students cut classes? Why are
          students not worried about low grades?" [What] really

stood out is that [students say they] don't care about low grades because their parents don't care. That's what stood out—that parents don't care.

....

Mrs. A: Well, the survey came up because we are finding that many of our students don't like math and the reasons they don't like math are two different extremes. Parents didn't have success in math or parents had success in math pushing the children and the children are not willing to accept. So it's those two extremes. There really don't seem to be a middle ground. The survey was to help us to come up with some ideas that might help us to better serve the students that we don't seem to be able to reach in either category. . . . Basically, many of the kids were saying that their parents didn't care. . . . I don't know how much that is true in terms of whether or not the parents have *told* them they don't care. However, I do know that for the number of students that make D's and F's in the math classes, we should see many more parents coming to the schools looking at what we're doing, asking questions.

Although these comments do not provide any real substantiation of whether parents did or did not care about their children's education, Mrs. Allgood raises an interesting and obvious question: If so many of the students at Hillside were not doing well, why weren't there more parents expressing concern and showing up at the school? Part of the reason concerned the additional obligations and economic realities that many parents faced. Despite their critical comments about parents, the math teachers were also sympathetic to these day-to-day problems that can sometimes stand in the way of parents being able to make their way into the schools or monitor the progress of their children:

Mr. O: There are some parents who care so much about their kids. Again, you have a lot of parents today, the parents who are just so young. They are sometimes at the level of their kids in thinking, endurance, and all of that. If you have a parent who doesn't have that determination to just go and succeed, then what kind of example are you showing. A lot of our kids have those kind of parents. There are parents who would like to be there, help their kids do all these things but due to economic pressure that is on them they have to pay bills. They have to pay rent and all that. Therefore they have to have a job, two jobs. After all of this, there's no

> time left to do parenting. Being there for the kid. If you ask
> them for their own reasons, they have good ones for not
> being there.

Despite these obligations, we must be concerned about the fact that students may, in fact, interpret their parents' absence as a sign of not caring. For me, the potentially devastating effects of these beliefs on students' mathematics achievement and persistence are clear: Mathematics learning and knowledge may come to be considered not important by many students. This was true for a majority of students at Hillside.

DISCUSSION

The school, classroom, and curricular conditions found at Hillside were far from ideal. In fact, they were very complex and unpredictable. Although teachers developed a vision of what they wanted to accomplish for their students and set specific goals in this regard, several complicating factors, having to do with student culture, curricular change, and community forces and beliefs about mathematics, brought about a different reality. How did these factors contextualize the underachievement and low motivation that was common to many students at Hillside and account for the apparent lack of fit between teacher expectations and goals and student expectations and goals?

First, community forces did play a role in many students' mathematics socializations. Although the mathematics teachers at Hillside believed that these forces were a major factor in both student success and failure, my observations showed that many students assigned little importance or instrumental value to mathematics learning. One reason for this was revealed by students themselves. When they were asked about the factors that caused some students to achieve below their potential or suffer from low motivation, the most common factors cited were lack of parental support and interest. Many parents simply stayed away from Hillside because of oppositional relationships with teachers and school officials, their own fears of mathematics, or larger socioeconomic concerns that demanded more of their attention. We also need to consider the fact that although parents and community members can make pro-mathematics statements, indicating that it is an important school subject and that they want their children to do well, the legacy of their own mathematics experiences can sometimes unwittingly undermine these sentiments.

Parents may not have intended to send the message that their children's mathematical activities were unimportant, but many students apparently interpreted their parents' absence to mean this. Harold's narrative serves as a good example of this unintended effect.

Second, it was also true that the norms that defined the dominant student culture at Hillside were too strong for some students to overcome. Being in middle school, students were at an especially critical time in their mathematics socializations and academic and adolescent development. Many were confronted with some very tough choices and questions: Do I want to be considered smart and risk ridicule from my peers? Am I willing to ask for help and appear that I don't know what's going on? Why should I bother learning these new ways of doing math? When am I ever going to use this? Unfortunately, a majority of students were not able to respond effectively to these questions or engage in behaviors that promoted their success. Many, in fact, engaged in "acting up" as described by Mr. Olander earlier in this chapter.

Third, the mathematics teachers at Hillside could not perform as effectively as they would have liked, or planned to, in their roles as agents of mathematics socialization. The small amount of data that I presented on their personal histories, their teaching philosophies, their beliefs about the role and importance of education, and their beliefs about their students and students' parents provided additional insight into their actions within the classroom context. These data also helped point out that what teachers do in their classrooms, what they believe about their students, and the content decisions they make are affected by factors that extend beyond the school and classroom context. Teachers bring with them a wealth of background and experiential resources from outside the school context. They interact with their students in ways that are indicative of their attempts to reconcile these personal experiences and beliefs with those of their students. The teachers' role in the students' mathematics socializations, then, is characterized by a complexity that extends well beyond simple notions of differential treatment based on students' racial and socioeconomic background. Moreover, despite their best efforts and intentions to steer students in the right direction, provide meaningful mathematical activities, and promote positive messages about mathematics, teachers were not the sole arbiters of what happened in their classrooms. The reality was that Mrs. Allgood and her students had to negotiate the mathematical and social norms that defined their classrooms. According to Mr. Olander, this negotiation process took up valuable class time and, in the end, there were often huge differences between what teachers and students believed about the nature, purpose, and importance of their classroom and curricular practices.

Finally, it is helpful to consider the curriculum chosen for use in the seventh-grade classrooms. This curriculum was intended to build on aspects of students' real-world experiences and to make mathematics more meaningful for them. Yet, the curriculum was met with resistance from students because of the ways in which it challenged their conceptions about what counts as mathematics and what it means to do mathematics. Students had spent the previous 6 years of their lives doing mathematics in a more or less traditional manner. Many had become comfortable with these old ways of doing mathematics and had developed certain expectations about what kinds of activities were appropriate for math class. The Algebra Project curriculum and what it demanded from students violated these expectations and caused many students to openly question whether what they were doing was in fact "real" mathematics. The result was disruptive days like those days described earlier in this chapter.

4

"Because I Want to Be Somebody:"

African-American Student Narratives on Academic and Mathematics Success

Although several school and community-level factors caused many students at Hillside to experience low motivation and underachievement, students at Hillside also had opportunities to learn. This chapter gives voice to a group of students who were able to take advantage of these opportunities and achieve academic and mathematics success. Narratives from seven students are presented. These narratives will be used to elaborate the themes that comprise the third level of the multilevel framework that I introduced in chapter 1. Those themes are reproduced in Table 4.1.

TABLE 4.1
Fourth Level of Multilevel Framework

Agency and Mathematics Success
Among African-American Students

- Personal identities and goals

- Perceptions of school climate, peers, and teachers

- Beliefs about mathematics abilities and motivation to learn

- Beliefs about instrumental importance of mathematics knowledge

- Beliefs about differential treatment from peers

A major goal of this chapter is to highlight the often overlooked strengths and resiliency of African-American students, particularly in mathematics. Researchers outside the field of mathematics education have, for example, focused on family socialization patterns to determine African-American parents' contributions to their children's school success (e.g., Clark, 1984). Other researchers have identified several educational strategies used by students themselves to achieve and maintain their academic success. Ogbu (1989a, 1989b), in particular, has described a set of strategies used by some successful African-American students: emulation of Whites, cultural passing, accommodation without assimilation, mentoring, attending private schools, and secretly doing one's work at home. Other scholars (e.g., Fordham, 1988) have identified students who camouflage their success by adopting raceless personas whereby they relinquish aspects of their African-American identity and culture, such as speech and language patterns, in favor of conforming to mainstream ideals and images of success. I do not question the existence of these strategies, but I believe appeals to these strategies as the cause of Black student success are limited in explanatory scope. Many African-American students openly embrace academic success without fear of reprisal from their peers and often achieve their successes by utilizing the same strategies as successful students from other ethnic groups. Moreover, African-American students, like these other students, often belong to or form peer groups in which success does not take on negative connotations.

Within mathematics education, African-American student success has received relatively little attention (e.g., Clewell, Anderson, & Thorpe, 1992; Silver, Smith, & Nelson, 1995; Treisman, 1985). Instead, most studies have focused on student failure, often reporting this failure in aggregate form with little attention or voice given to the individual African-American students in those studies.

Few studies inside or outside of mathematics education have focused on African-American students' agency-related behaviors or the degree to which knowledge of certain subjects is viewed as essential to achieving their goals (e.g., Nieto, 1996; O'Connor, 1997; Treisman, 1985). In this chapter, I examine both individual agency and mathematics identity among African-American students. My discussion focuses on the ways in which successful students view themselves as learners of mathematics, the beliefs they hold about the instrumental importance of mathematics, their motivations to learn mathematics, and the actions they take to achieve and maintain their success.

I interviewed 35 high-achieving seventh-, eighth-, and ninth-grade African-American students at Hillside. I selected these 35 students after observing them for a few months in their mathematics classrooms, in the context of school events, and going to and coming from class. Although their grades in mathematics were not all A's, these students did perform at a level that differentiated them from their peers, both socially and mathematically. The personal backgrounds of these students did not fit one particular profile. Some of the students were from single-parent families, some from two-parent families. Others were living with relatives. Also, the socioeconomic backgrounds of the students showed great variation, ranging from those students having parents or guardians with professional jobs to those whose parents or guardians were out of the labor force due to unemployment, disability, or retirement. This variation among the students also highlights the various sources of and influences on their agency. What were these sources? Theoretically, Bandura's (1982, 1986, 1997) work on personal efficacy broadly characterizes many of them. Bandura identified four such sources: (1) *mastery experiences* which provide direct evidence of whether one can succeed, (2) *vicarious experiences* provided by social models and people similar to themselves who persevere to success or who fail despite high effort, (3) *social persuasion*, in the form of verbal messages that one can or cannot succeed, and (4) *physiological and affective states* that lead to judgments about one's capabilities, strengths, and vulnerabilities. In many ways, these terms describe general aspects of the processes that influence students' mathematics socializations and the construction of their mathematics identities. These terms also describe some of the dynamics of the agency model that I presented in Figure 1.2. In the narratives presented below, these general terms are fleshed out in ways that speak to the particular experiences of mathematically successful African American students. A number of other sources of these students' agencies also will be discussed in this chapter.

The seven students profiled in this chapter include two ninth-graders, three eighth-graders, and two seventh-graders. Five are girls and two are boys. Each of the ninth-grade students and one of the eighth-graders were enrolled in geometry, an accelerated class. The other eighth-grade student was enrolled in algebra. Each of the seventh-grade students was enrolled in the Algebra Project. The lowest grade-point-average achieved among the seven at any time during the year was 3.33. Some had maintained 4.0 grade-point-averages during one or more marking periods.

As was the case with parents and community members in chapter 2, my discussion of mathematics socialization and identity among these students is embedded within discussions of their larger personal and academic identities. Readers will also note that different themes predominate in the different cases—mathematics was not always front and center. Some of the students did use the opportunity to discuss why they believe mathematics is important and why their future plans depended on knowledge of mathematics. Others used the interview to discuss the pain caused by differential treatment from their peers as a result of their "good student" status. Still others talked about how their life circumstances—good and bad—outside of school served as motivation to do well. In addition, readers will see that several factors helped motivate students, including family and teacher support, outside interests such as sports, goals of making a lot of money, and the need to help others through community service.

One limitation of the student narratives is that I did not explicitly discuss issues of race, class, and gender or seek students' beliefs about the possible constraints in life as a result of their African-American or gender status. At each of the grade levels, there was a very noticeable gender gap in the number of successful students. Girls outnumbered boys in many classes and did much better academically. Other researchers (e.g., Fordham, 1993; Schultz, 1996) have studied academic achievement among African-American females and the special issues they face. I did not explore those factors because gender issues did not arise as a topic of discussion in the interviews.

Moreover, although I was able to clearly identify relationships between the mathematics identities and African-American identities of parents and community members, these relationships did not arise to any great extent in my discussions with students. One of the students did refer to the fact that her desire to attend Harvard University was based on a need to prove that African-Americans were capable of doing so. I suspect that the other students were aware of the racial disparities that exist in society and the meaning and role of their African-American status in their life chances. I also suspect that the strength of these students' personal identities would have caused many of them to use their recognition of the potential barriers in society and the negative experiences of their parents and other members of their communities as sources of personal motivation.

In terms of their mathematical socializations, each of the 35 students was exposed to a variety of messages about education and mathematics. These messages came from teachers, parents, and peers. These students, unlike their less successful peers, were very adept at navigating their way through these mixed messages. Where positive messages prevailed, these students utilized them in ways that assisted them in their goals and strengthened their beliefs in themselves and their efforts. Where negative messages prevailed, these students were able to overcome their possible effects by adopting personal philosophies such as "Kick it out of the way and keep on going" or "Just let it go in one ear and out the other."

Because the seven profiled students came from a range of family backgrounds and socioeconomic levels, it is clear that their success was not determined solely by their sociodemographic characteristics or family structures. Their success was also affected by motivational and dispositional factors. In this regard, these mathematically successful students, like the complete collection of 35, shared a number of characteristics and traits. First, all of these students demonstrated high levels of achievement-oriented individual agency and bold defiance of the negative influences that surrounded them. In particular, I found that they engaged in what might be termed *self-definition by opposition*, resisting not only the dominant underachievement norms that existed among their peers but also those negative elements of their community that are often thought of as inescapable or ensuring failure. Moreover, rather than cite only the aid and encouragement of their teachers and parents as important factors in their success, these students attributed much of their success to their own efforts and strong personal identities. They had developed clear and focused short-term and long-term goals that they believed would not be possible without education.

Second, nearly all of the students expressed high levels of confidence in their mathematics abilities. They also expressed positive valuations of mathematics, considering mathematics a valuable school subject and important for instrumental reasons. Not all of these students identified mathematics as their favorite subject, but they still considered mathematical knowledge a necessary ingredient to achieving their goals and future success. In class, these students acted on their spoken beliefs by completing their assignments on time and doing what was asked of them, even though they occasionally complained of boredom or that the subject matter was too easy.[4]

Third, many of the students characterized their teachers in a positive light, showed appreciation for their efforts, believed they were interested in helping students learn, and thought they were helpful toward this end. However, these students also displayed a willingness to be critical of their teachers. Many characterized particular teachers

---

[4] It is interesting to note that many low-achieving students also expressed high levels of confidence in their abilities and held the belief that mathematics is an important school subject. However, when I observed them in their classrooms, these students' actions often went against their spoken beliefs. These actions often resulted in an agency that was mostly negative and detrimental to their progress.

as too boring and not challenging. Despite these complaints, successful students, unlike many of their peers, did not let their critical perceptions of their teachers stand in the way of their learning.

Fourth, and probably most disheartening, I found that despite their success and positive valuations of themselves, education, and mathematics, nearly all of the successful students cited some form of differential treatment from their peers. This usually took the form of good-natured teasing, such as being called "nerd" but also included more serious taunts such as accusations of trying to "act White." Some researchers (e.g., Fordham, 1988; Fordham & Ogbu, 1986) have interpreted these more serious attacks as representing challenges to the ethnic and cultural identities of successful African-American students. These taunts may also reveal an underlying belief in some African-American peer groups that some behaviors, such as speaking standard English, are considered inappropriate or "White" behaviors and that engaging in such behaviors should be avoided. If similar beliefs are found to hold for mathematics learning, then it would seem that mathematically successful African-American students must make serious decisions about crossing these so-called "cultural boundaries."

As readers make their way through the cases, questions may arise about my characterizations of these students and the reasons for their success. A particularly important question concerns my assumptions about the primacy of mathematical knowledge and mathematics success in the lives of these students. The concept of *success*, as I had initially considered it, connoted students receiving high grades in mathematics and expressing positive attitudes about mathematics learning. But my conceptualization of their success expanded as I analyzed their stories in more detail. It expanded beyond consideration of their mathematical behaviors to include their exemplary social behaviors including the fact that they were able to resist the antiachievement norms that defined the attitudes and behaviors of many students at Hillside. This expanded definition was also necessary because although some of the students regarded mathematics as their favorite subject, so important that they did not want to "risk not knowing" it, not all of these students did so.

This last observation raises interesting questions about the role and importance of mathematics identity in students' success. Were the positive mathematics identities of these students at the core of their success? Or did each student possess such a strong overall academic identity that doing well in mathematics was just a part of that? My tendency to orient the discussion in the direction of the first possibility is given support by the fact that some students did regard mathematics as their favorite subject and appeared to rely on their mathematics success as motivation to do well in other classes. Yet, this notion is challenged by the fact that some students did not regard math as their favorite subject and elected to do well in it only because they were motivated to maintain their status and identity as top students. Given these competing explanations, readers may ask for a reconciliation.

As each case is read, I urge that the following be kept in mind: Both processes for manufacturing and maintaining success—constructing a strong math identity that fuels a strong student identity and constructing a strong student identity that motivates one to do well in math—are productive and positive and can only benefit students. The important point to consider, particularly for mathematics educators, is that mathematics plays a central role in each. If African-American students develop strong academic identities that encourage high achievement, they may be motivated to do well in mathematics. If students draw strength from their success in mathematics, then they may be motivated to do well in other subjects as well.

Of course, neither the seven cases nor the complete collection of 35 capture all aspects of what it meant to be an African-American student at Hillside or in general. In addition, this small number of cases cannot describe the mathematics experiences of all African-American students. In that regard, the vignettes presented here will not lead to a prescription or list of suggestions for how African-American students can insure their success. Nevertheless, the stories of the seven profiled students are informative because they offer compelling examples of how success can be found within a diversity of African-American student backgrounds. One of my main goals in giving these students voice is to bring to life what academic and mathematics success meant to them in the context of the community and school forces that they encountered—both positive and negative. By considering the particular stories of these seven successful students and how the students negotiated community and school forces, we gain a better understanding of how these forces can serve as barriers or springboards to success.

LISA: "BECAUSE I WANT TO BE SOMEBODY"

This narrative is from Lisa, a 14-year-old African-American female at the time of the interview. Lisa lives in Oakland with her parents and her older sister. Her sister was attending high school as a tenth-grader. Her mother, who has a master's degree, splits her employment between working as a substitute teacher in the Oakland Unified School

District and as a home health aide. Lisa's father also attended college and owns a trucking company in a nearby city. Lisa was in the eighth grade at the time of her interview and was enrolled in the accelerated track in mathematics. She made the honor roll every marking period during the year of the study. She was a very outgoing young lady and could always be seen carrying an armload of books as well as a book bag on her back. She often participated in math contests sponsored by the math department at Hillside and won several of them. During her interview, Lisa indicated that math was her favorite subject—although she liked all of her classes—and that she especially liked her math teachers because they were always teaching her something new.

Like many of the successful students in the study, Lisa possessed a very positive personal identity. She saw herself as very intelligent, hardworking, and goal-oriented, and she took an interest in subjects that many of her peers did not. Rather than adopt an "I don't care" attitude, as many of her peers appeared to do, Lisa felt the need to keep struggling in order to reach her goals:

DM: How would you describe yourself as a person?

L: I would describe myself as very intelligent, smart, outgoing, and very interested in learning certain things. . . . I like to do a lot of things that other people might consider boring or not fun such as math. A lot of people don't like math but I happen to like math. Because at this grade level, most people drop out or their grades might be up and they go down because they get to a point where they just don't care anymore. But me, I'm just kind of struggling to keep going.

DM: How would you describe yourself as a student?

L: Hardworking. Wanting to meet certain points. I would also consider myself intelligent, responsible.

....

DM: What kind of "points" do you want to reach?

L: Like by the time I get into high school, I want to go through geometry. Know a lot about science. I would like to know all of it. I would like to be advanced. I feel that if you want to get through this world, you must know a lot.

Personal Goals and Motivation to Learn

As indicated by her comments, part of Lisa's motivation for wanting to succeed, as well for adopting such a strong sense-of-self, was that she wanted to be someone special. Her idea of being special was to become a teacher because she felt the need to convey her personal philosophy about success and the importance of schooling to other students:

DM: Why do you say that [you have to keep struggling to go on]?

L: Because I want to be somebody. I want to be someone. Not just drop out of school, get pregnant, be on welfare. I want to depend on myself, have a job, a family. I know if I don't go to school, whatever I plan will not come true. If you don't go to school, you won't achieve what you want to be in the future. That's the reason.

DM: Did somebody tell you that?

L: It's my image of what I believe. I want to be someone important. Very important. Famous. I want to be a teacher. I want to be a teacher because I can get the message across to younger people while they're still young and as they get older, they'll learn to know right from wrong.

....

DM: How far do you want to go in school?

L: I want to go all the way through high school, through college, and teaching. But there's only one life. You only live once and I want to become a whole lot of things.

Lisa's goals also reflected a great deal of individual agency on her part. She acknowledged the support of parents and family but was also willing to give herself credit. In addition, her comments revealed that her larger sense-of-self was connected to her performance in school:

DM: What makes you stay on track?

L: My parents encourage me. . . . I would say my whole family. They're like, "We know you can go through school. We know you can do it. All you have to do is make it through

high school and go to college and get you a good job, a
decent house, and go on about business." They just
encourage me all the way. . . . [But] basically, it's just me.
Me wanting to be somebody. I know if I want to become
whatever I want to become, you have to have school. So I
just stay on track. Think about school.

....

DM: What do you usually shoot for in terms of your grades? A's
        and B's? Are you happy with a C?

L: A C is like no credit with me. D, F, C. It don't go with me.

DM: What would happen if you got a D or F?

L: I would be mad. But you work for what you deserve. I know
        I don't deserve a D or F. I would go back to that teacher
        and say that I think you made a mistake, could you please
        check this. If I got a D or an F, I wouldn't take my report
        card home.

Perceptions of School Climate and Peers

Lisa realized that the kinds of goals she set for herself and the kinds of
beliefs that she adopted set her apart from most of her peers. Although
she was very well aware of her surroundings at school and the potential
to fall in with the wrong crowd, she was able to develop a strong,
internal disposition to succeed. Lisa commented on the environment
at Hillside in a way that showed her displeasure with some of the
other students:

DM: Is there a worst part of the school year or stuff that you
        don't quite like?

L: As you see, there's a lot of people that just don't really care
        anymore. They may even curse the teacher or even act up
        when the principal or someone isn't here.

DM: Why do you think some of the kids do stuff like that?

L   I don't know. They just want attention.

DM: Do you think there are more kids that are like that in school,
        or more kids that are not like that?

L: I would say there are more kids that are like that.

....

DM: Do you think other kids think like you?

L: No. Because most people don't care about school. Like some people cut [classes]. I don't see a point to cut. I don't see a point at all.

DM: Why do you think other kids don't quite think the same way you do?

L: I don't think they do. They just don't care. That's it.

The fact that Lisa differentiated her peers along lines of achievement and motivation confirms observations made by teachers as well as by myself. As I indicated in chapter 3, there appeared to be two major student groups at Hillside: a large group of underachievers and a smaller group of high-achievers. Lisa recognized this division as well:

DM: Let's say you met somebody and they wanted to know about your school. How would you describe it here?

L: Some kids are very outgoing. They like to be with certain groups. Some kids like to be with the bad group. There's a bad side and there's a good side. If you choose to be on the bad side, then go ahead. That's just going to make you look worse. The nice people are usually the people with a 3.0 or whatever. When some kids come here, they began to hang out with them. Later on, when someone on the bad side comes along and starts talking to them, getting into their minds, starts possessing them. . . . They'll go along with them and [later] wish they would have been with someone else.

Because she had a strong awareness of the potential negative effects of peer pressure, Lisa did not let the actions of students around her affect her personal goals. Lisa was also able to comment on many of the other students at Hillside and whether she perceived them as liking math as much as she did. In her opinion, most of the students did not:

DM: When you are in your classes, what kind of stuff is going on? How are the other kids behaving?

L: It depends on what classes. In some classes, they're quiet. Most of the classes, they don't do their work. They're rowdy. They like to throw papers. Talk back to the teachers. Disrespect. . . . Some of them are just illiterate. They're out of it.

DM: What are you doing when all this stuff is going on?

L: Just doing my work.

. . . .

DM: If you could make any changes, what would you change?

L: What would I change about the school? First of all, I would change people's attitudes. Second, I would change the way they speak to the teachers and other people.

Although Lisa had mostly negative perceptions of her peers, their lack of motivation, and their effects on other students, she had mostly positive comments about her teachers, particularly her math teachers:

DM: Is there a best part about this year?

L: Yeah, there's a whole lot. . . . Especially I like my math teachers. The math teachers are it. They teach me certain things that I know I have to have if I go to Geometry. . . . The teachers are very nice. Don't listen to rumors about what students say about teachers such as that teacher is mean or that teacher will give you a bad grade if you don't do this or do that. . . . Just don't listen.

Mathematics Identity: Beliefs About Mathematical Ability

Lisa's strong personal identity and her ability to recognize the forces around her also affected her beliefs about her mathematics ability. She identified mathematics as her favorite subject, partly because of the teachers but also because of the subject matter. She was considered by all of the math teachers to be an excellent math student. Doing well in mathematics, as in her other courses, seemed to be so tightly intertwined with her personal identity that she felt bad when she didn't meet her expectations:

DM: Do you consider yourself to be a top student?

L: I consider myself in between. Even top in some areas.

DM: What have your GPA's been?

L: 4.0, 3.65, 3.83.

DM: What are your favorite classes?

L: Math, science, English, all of them. I don't have any classes that I don't like. I like math the best of all. It's like a maze, it's like having fun but you're learning at the same time.

DM: You've gotten all A's and B's in that class?

L: In the beginning of the year, I got a C. One C. That was the only C I received. That wasn't satisfying to me. I feel that if I got a C, I wasn't trying hard enough or I wasn't showing him that I could do something. So, I used to just get my mind straight on math. That's it, math. Having dreams about math. I come back and I would get an A on my test.

                ....

DM: Do you usually feel challenged in your math class?

L: I feel it's challenging. I like challenges.

DM: Do you ever give up?

L: I don't give up. Never. Never give up. If you give up it's sort of like saying I don't care or it doesn't matter. I don't feel that way. I don't give up at all. Whatever it is. Even if it's not related to school, I don't give up.

                ....

DM: I know that you said that you like math. Are you *good* at it?

L: Sort of. Like if we do a review, I know that already. If we're going to go ahead in the chapter, then I already know how to do it. So I just glance through the book. When I don't have anything to do on the weekends, I just go through the math book. Some people [say], "She's a nerd. She spends her time in the books." But I consider myself good in math.

Mathematics Identity: Beliefs About
the Importance of Mathematics

Lisa's earlier comments made it clear that she wanted to do well academically and that she especially wanted to do well in mathematics. Not only did she recognize mathematics as an important school subject but she was able to focus on its instrumental value and how it could help her achieve her future goals:

DM: Do you want to take more math classes? Next year you said you want to take geometry. Do you think you can do geometry?

L: Well, actually think I do. Because if I know algebra, then I should be able to do geometry because algebra is going to help me do geometry and I want geometry because I know that's the next step.

....

D: You said you wanted to be a teacher?

L: I want to be a teacher. If I don't become a teacher, I would like to become a doctor or a veterinarian or a computer analyst.

D: Do you think you'll need math to do that stuff?

L: I think you'll need math. Of course. No math, no job. No good job. Work at McDonald's. You still need math for that.

....

DM: Is math important to you or is it just like another subject?

L: It's like another subject but it's also important. I know that if I don't have math, no job. . . . . It's just the way I think.

....

DM: Are there some kids that don't like math?

L: That's more than half the school. If they really cared about what they're doing, you would see it. If they were really interested in school you would notice it. They would go straight to class.

Beliefs About Differential Treatment

Although she was very successful in her academic efforts and set very high goals for herself, Lisa admitted that she sometimes faced differential treatment from her peers. This treatment came in the form of name-calling and accusations of being a nerd. However, she did not let this stand in her way because she maintained a support group of friends who thought like her and ignored or avoided those who did not:

DM: What kind of group do you hang around with?

L: Smart people. Good people. I say that because they're not involved in any bad things. They like to do things. They're smart. They try to encourage each other, make the right decisions. They're not nerds. I would say that I hang out with a good group of people.

DM: People call you nerd?

L: They call everybody nerd. It can even be a friend. Like if you get a 3.0 or over, they'll say she's just a nerd or he's just a nerd. . . . He or she is the teacher's pet. . . . I'm just a person just like you are. It's just that I like to succeed.

....

DM: You mentioned some of the stuff that people do. They may curse at the teacher or call people nerd. Does that get in your way?

L: That don't get in my way. I just keep stepping. It's just like trash. Kick it out the way and keep going. . . . If you let it stop you, there's no point in continuing what you're doing. That's the way I see it.

PAULETTE: "I CARE ABOUT MY EDUCATION NOW MORE THAN ANYTHING"

Paulette was a 15-year-old ninth-grader at the time of this interview. She has 13 brothers and sisters and lives in Oakland with one of her older sisters who is a psychologist at a local hospital. Of all the students at Hillside, Paulette may have been the most celebrated. She graduated from ninth grade having received the outstanding student award in several areas. In addition, her teachers spoke favorably about her at all times. Her achievements were all the more noteworthy given that in seventh grade she was, by her own admission, headed down the wrong path. However, after reassessing her direction in life and her goals, she turned her academic life around to the point where she was able to enroll in the accelerated track in mathematics and to maintain a perfect grade-point-average during the last half of her ninth-grade year.

Personal Identity

Paulette, like Lisa, possessed a very strong personal identity. She had clear short-term and long-term goals and believed that she would achieve them through hard work. She was forthright about giving herself credit for making adjustments in her life that would make her goals and dreams become reality:

DM: How would you describe yourself as a person?

P: I would describe myself as a hardworking, outgoing, intelligent, respectful. . . . At school, I'm not involved too much but I do tutor after school for Mr. Olander and throughout the week I work.

DM: How would you describe yourself as a student?

P: Hardworking. Willing to learn more and listen. Smart.

                          ....

DM: You do consider yourself to be smart?

P: Yes, I consider myself smart. Well, this year I really got into my grades, really cared about what my grades were. In seventh grade, I was getting like 2.17 but now I got 4.0 straight. [Back] then I was really worried about hanging with my friends. I was more involved in play. But now I realize it's coming close for me to graduate and then I'll be in high school next year and it's not really time for play anymore. So I started working harder and getting my grades together. Last semester, my average was a 3.67. That was my average. This semester, hopefully it will be a 4.0. These last two marking periods, I had 4.0's. I believe I can do it again. If I do it this last time, then it'll be a 4.0 average.

Paulette strongly believed that education was the key to achieving her goals. Unlike many of the students at Hillside, Paulette did not succumb to negative peer pressure and allow it affect her motivation and behavior. Recognizing that many of her old friends had interfered with her ability to succeed, she changed her criteria for selecting her friends—shifting her focus from being surrounded by people with whom she could have fun to those who were academically successful:

DM: Have you always liked school?

P: I love school. I care about my education now more than anything. So, I love school. . . . Because without education, you'll live in poverty. You'll really have nothing. You can't really get nowhere being unintelligent.

DM: Did somebody tell you that or is that what you know?

P: That's what I know.

....

DM: You can look back on eighth grade and seventh grade and see how you changed. Are you much different?

P: I changed. I'm much different. I always got good grades but the kind of friends I hung around I didn't want to show them that I was too smart. I wouldn't come to class a few times. I knew I was always smart. Well, everyone knew I was smart. It was fun hanging around my friends but that distracted me from my work.

DM: Do you still have those same friends?

P: No. I changed friends altogether. . . . I pick my friends on their personality first. Their [behavior] and then their grades. I got to really know a person. See where their mind is at.

Personal Goals and Motivation to Learn

A common trait among the successful students that I interviewed was that their larger senses of self appeared to be closely tied to their academic identities. Paulette was no exception. Doing well in school had a definite impact on how she saw herself and the beliefs she formed about her abilities:

DM: What grades do you usually shoot for?

P: I always shoot for As.

DM: Would you settle for Cs?

P: I wouldn't settle. Most people say if it's a B, that's good.
        But I know I'm better than a B, so I want an A. Because I
        know what I'm capable of. I know I can do good work and
        try harder.

....

DM: Let's say you got all Fs in your classes. How would you
        feel?

P: I would feel really ignorant. Low. My self-esteem would be
        low. I'd feel that I couldn't go any further. But it would also
        make me want to try harder.

Paulette was highly motivated to be successful not only in school
but in life. Her motivation went well beyond a desire for material gain
and revealed a strong desire combat many of the negative conditions
that existed in her community. Because of this, she began to develop
an early sense of service and a desire to help those around her:

DM: What's the difference between you and some of the people
        who are not really doing well?

P: I think it has a lot to do with the person that I am. Where I
        want to get to in life. I know what's ahead. I think I'm on
        the right track [because of] my religion. Second, my goals.
        What I expect in life and what I want. It's a need for me to
        be successful. That's what I want to do. My ambition is to
        help people. When I go downtown and the people I see in
        poverty. I don't feel we should live like that. So, if I'm
        successful then I know I can help somebody else be
        successful.

....

DM: What's pushing you?

P: I want to be successful. That's my main goal and I know
        what I have to do to be successful. I really want to be a

psychiatrist. I really want to deal with the human mind to see how people react in their behavior and I want to help people.

Perceptions of Peers and School Climate

Like Lisa, Paulette was very critical of her peers. She clearly made an effort to distance herself from them and often referred to their disruptive behavior and apparent lack of goals as the antithesis of what she wanted for herself:

DM: How would you describe this school to somebody on the outside?

P: It's violent. Boring. Maybe because I'm more mature than others. I don't really relate to the students. . . . They're violent, disrespectful, rude. It's a few good ones. A few that do care about their education. But the majority runs on violence. Negative, very negative. They go around writing on walls, cursing, setting off fire alarms.

....

DM: So you think there's more of the negative people and just a smaller group of people that are on track? Why do you think the other group is so big?

P: Because that group are friends. They hang around each other. It's the influence that they're under. They probably like doing what they do because they don't understand. Ten years from now, what will [they] be doing 10 years from now. Living the life that they're living, they'll be doing nothing. They'll probably be somewhere on the streets. They really don't understand the concept of life.

Perceptions of Teachers

Paulette was also willing to be critical of her teachers. Most notably, she criticized some of them for their inability to discipline certain students and keep control of their classrooms. She saw this as interfering with other students' ability to learn. She did admire those teachers who were able and willing to keep students under control and create a classroom atmosphere conducive to learning:

DM: How would you describe the teachers?

P: It's a few here that discipline. Not many. I like them. They're okay.

DM: You mentioned discipline a couple of times. Why do you think that's important?

P: If a student comes in to class and they figure they can do anything they want, then that distracts the other students. If everybody is doing work and everybody is learning then that'll be an influence on them. But if it's a lot of noise and confusion and throwing paper, then everybody will get involved.

....

DM: What are your favorite classes?

P: Geometry and art. I say art because it's not really the work that we do. It's the teacher himself. He disciplines a lot. Most students here, they really run over the teachers and are real disrespectful. But he demands respect. I admire him for that. Geometry, I learn a lot. It's like I'm constantly learning in class. It's not boring.

Mathematics Identity: Beliefs About Mathematical Ability

Paulette's strong personal and academic identities encapsulated her strong mathematics identity. She expressed very few doubts about her mathematical ability and she considered herself at the top of her geometry class. She identified mathematics as her favorite subject and believed that she understood and knew what she was doing. She was so good at mathematics that she was selected to be a tutor, a responsibility that she agreed to accept despite demanding school and work schedules:

DM: Let me ask you about your math class. . . . Has it been one of your best subjects?

P: Math has been my *best* subject. Math has *always* been my best subject. . . . I tutor algebra. So that gives me a better understanding of what I missed last year. On Monday nights, I'll go home and look over what it is that they have to do. If I don't understand, then I may take an hour or two hours to understand it. So it gives me a better understanding also. I get home from work at about 8 [PM] at night. From 8 [PM] to sometimes 12 [AM], I'm studying and doing homework.

....

DM: Do you think you're good at math?

P: Yes. Because I understand it and when tests come I'm not really lost or anything. When the test comes, I can just go through it.

DM: Do you like other people to think that you're good at math?

P: Yes. I don't want to be looked at as a bad person. I like someone to see significance in me.

....

DM: Would you put yourself at the top, middle, bottom?

P: I put myself at the top. . . . Because I go for the best. I'm a hard worker. Whatever is right, then that's what I want. I want what's right.

Perceptions of Differential Treatment

Like most of the students profiled in this chapter, Paulette cited some form of differential treatment from her peers. However, she did not let it affect her or stand in her way. As I observed her over the course of several months, I noticed that Paulette maintained small friendship groups and that she did not interact with many of the students who were considered disruptive. She informed me that some of these students were former friends who now treated her differently:

DM: What do the other kids say about the fact that you do well.

P: A few of them, they're happy. They congratulate me. But some of my former friends, I don't really let this get to me, but they may turn their nose up at me. They may speak to me but if I was to glance at them, their nose is turned up at me. It don't bother me. . . . I know by being the person that I am, I'll be successful. If they have an attitude like that, they're not going to get nowhere.

ANNETTE: "I LIKE MATH. I CAN JUST SEE IT SOMETIMES. IT JUST COMES TO ME ALL OF A SUDDEN."

Annette was a 14-year-old eighth-grader at the time of this interview. She lives in Oakland with her parents and has one younger sister. Her mother works for a shipping company and her father works for the city of Oakland as a computer programmer. Her mother completed 1 year of college and her father completed 4 years. Of all the students at Hillside, Annette was the most advanced in her mathematics courses. She was 1 year ahead of schedule and was the only eighth-grade student enrolled in geometry. During the year of the study, her lowest grade point average for any of the marking periods was 3.85.

Annette described herself in a way that conveyed that she wanted to be thought of as hardworking and always trying to do her best. She also used these criteria to select her friends. Like Lisa and Paulette, much of her larger sense of self was connected to her academic performance. She believed that she should be achieving at a certain level and felt disappointed if she didn't maintain that level:

DM: How would you describe yourself as a person?

A: I make sure I get the job done whatever it is. . . . I volunteer for certain things. I'm in EAOP, Early Academic Outreach Program. I'm in CJSF, California Junior Scholarship Federation. I was in student union. . . . I have a lot of friends but I have about seven close friends and we always do stuff together. I'm not really shy but then I'm not outgoing. I'm a diligent student. Whenever I have a project due, I try to make it look the best that I can. I feel like I'm always competing with people trying to be the best. Whatever I do, I try to make it the best.

....

DM: How do you pick your friends?

A: I pick them out by looking at how well they do in school. What kind of things they do. I guess you can say I have all the smart people in my group. All of them are above 3.0.

Personal Goals and Motivation to Learn

Like Lisa and Paulette, Annette showed a strong resolve to succeed and attributed much of her success to her own efforts, agency, and beliefs:

DM: What makes you stay on track?

A: I know where I'm going. I know I'm going to go to college. I know that college is getting more expensive so I have to be the best or close to the best. . . . That's the way I am. It's not like my parents are pressuring me or my friends are pressuring me. It's just the way I feel. I think I'm kind of unique.

DM: Where do you get some of the motivation to do well?

A: It's me. I tell myself to do well. I can't stand B's.

Perceptions of Peers and School Climate

Annette did not have a favorable assessment of her peers, singling out large groups of students whose behaviors and attitudes she believed were disruptive to the learning environment at Hillside. She believed many of the students at Hillside did not care about their education and were not receiving the kind of support and encouragement from their parents and families that they needed to succeed:

DM: [There aren't a lot of students on the honor roll.] Why do you think you're one of the students that managed to get on that list?

A: I work hard and a lot of people don't care. It's not a big deal to them. . . . In general, a lot of people don't care. I pride myself on trying to stay up there. I feel so disappointed when I get a B in a class.

DM: Would you be happy with a C?

A: I've never had a C before in my life. A lot of people are happy if they get a C or a D. . . . I'm hardly happy with a B.

....

DM: Why do you think some of the kids don't care if they're not on the honor roll or if they don't get above a 2.0?

A: A lot of the people who don't care [their] home life is [not] too great. I hear some of them talking [about] what happened to them or their older brothers and sisters are doing something bad and they decide they want to be just like them. I think some of them are really smart but they don't come to class when they should.

....

DM: [If you could change anything about the students] what would you change?

A: I'd make them want to study more. Not cut so much. Change some of their attitudes. If you'd change that then it'd be perfect.

Perceptions of Teachers

Annette, like Paulette, was also critical of some of her teachers. She cited their inability to discipline some of the students and felt many teachers had to be "baby-sitters" for these disruptive students. On the other hand, when asked about her role models, she identified Mr. Olander:

DM: What are the teachers like?

A: Most of them are pretty good but some of them act like baby-sitters. They don't really teach. There are some who can't handle the classes and you don't really learn anything because they spend the whole time sending people to the office. . . . They have to spend all their time yelling at people and you only get 15 minutes of class.

....

DM: Do you have any role models?

A: I look up to my parents. Mr. Olander, my math teacher. Not really anybody else.

Mathematics Identity: Beliefs About Mathematical Ability

Annette clearly saw herself as a good mathematics student and had a high level of confidence in her ability. She ranked herself above other students and, in many ways, she was justified in doing so. She was, after all, the only eighth-grade student enrolled in geometry and would be the only student taking trigonometry in ninth grade. In order to do this, she would have to travel to a local high school and then return to Hillside to finish her day:

DM: Are you satisfied with how you're doing in math class?

A: I'm satisfied. I think I could do better. I feel like I'm slipping. It's not that anybody is going ahead of me. I feel like I could do better than I am.

DM: Have you maintained all A's in math?

A: All A's. The only class I got a B in was last year. That was because I messed up on a project.

....

D: Do you like math?

A: I like math. I can just see it sometimes. It just comes to me all of sudden. I'm looking at a problem and I know what the answer is. . . . Math is kind of easy to me. . . . But I think I'm doing okay. . . . I think I can do a lot of problems. Get most of them right.

....

D: What are you taking next year?

A: Trigonometry.

D: Who's going to teach that to you?

A: I'm going to [high school] and then I'm coming back here for the rest of the day.

D: Is anybody else in the school doing that?

A: No.

....

D: Where would you put yourself overall? In the top, the middle, at the bottom?

A: I don't want to sound vain but I think I'm in the top. . . . I do all my work and I usually get the highest grades. I pretty much know what I'm talking about most of the time.

Mathematics Identity: Beliefs About Importance of Mathematics

Because she participated in a number of enrichment programs and was aware of mathematical and scientific careers, it was not surprising that Annette realized the instrumental importance of mathematics and its relation to certain jobs:

DM: What are some of the reasons that you think you may need to learn [math]?

A: If I want to be a doctor or engineer. It'd be good to already have that under your belt.

DM: Did people tell you that or did you kind of know?

A: I kind of know that.

Beliefs About Differential Treatment

Because she was such a good student and was so far advanced in her mathematics, there was great potential for Annette to be ridiculed and called nerd by her peers—and she was. But, like Lisa and Paulette, she did not let negative comments and perceptions by others impede her progress toward her goals:

DM: Do people say any negative things [you being a good student]. Do people try and put you down?

A: Those are the type of people who don't usually do well in school. They're just doing that so they can feel better.

TERRELL: "WHY CAN'T I BE GOOD IN SCHOOL AND HAVE A GOOD SOCIAL LIFE?"

At the time of the interview, Terrell was a 14-year-old eighth-grader who lived with his father and grandmother in Oakland. He has six older sisters and one older brother. His father is a construction foreman.

According to Terrell, his father wanted to be a doctor but had to abandon plans to attend Stanford to take care of an ailing father. Before coming to Hillside, Terrell had attended local private schools.

Based on his grades and his behavior in his classroom, I knew that Terrell was a top mathematics student. But in our interview I also learned that he had several other interests. These interests were reflected in many different identities. Because we talked about each of these briefly, our interview did not focus very much on mathematics. Yet, there was no doubt that Terrell's academic and mathematics identities were closely related to the other identities he constructed.

What was most striking about Terrell's superior academic standing and his other successes was the negative treatment he received from his peers. Because of this mostly negative treatment, Terrell, like most of the successful students that I interviewed, developed a strong personal identity and sense of agency, giving himself credit for being able to withstand this treatment and for remaining committed to his success.

Personal Identity and Motivation to Learn

Of all the students that I interviewed, Terrell revealed what I believed to be the most complex personal identity. He had an outstanding academic record but, by his own admission, he was not as serious about school as he could have been. He simply worked hard when he had to. What motivated him was a desire to be "well rounded." He wanted to experience success in all areas of his life:

DM: How would you describe yourself as a person?

T: I would describe myself as a person who's not too wrapped up in my work. I get wrapped up in my work when I have to do it. When it comes down to it, I do my work. But I'm also there to have fun and enjoy myself. Because if I were there just to do my work all the time later on in life I might crack. I might just explode. I try to have fun too.

DM: How would you describe yourself as a student?

T: I don't like to rush things. I like to take my time. When I do it, I do it hard. I work hard and try my best all the time whenever I do my work. . . . I want to be well rounded. If I want to be good in sports, I want to also be good in school. Being well rounded, when I'm all grown up I can look back and say I did well in everything I did. I can't say I did bad in anything.

DM: Does that come from you or did somebody push you in that way? Where did that come from?

T: It comes from me mostly and also my mom and my dad inspired me to want to be like that. They do a little bit too much pushing but I can accept that because they want me to be the best I can be.

Personal Goals and Motivation to Learn

Because Terrell developed strong identities in several different areas, he was able to draw on his success in each of these areas. In addition to identifying himself as a good student he also took pride in being a good hockey player and used hockey as a primary motivation to do well in school. Terrell also indicated that he had a secret desire to be a writer. When I asked him to explain where his motivation came from to do well in the different areas of his life Terrell cited his own agency and determination but also indicated that he received encouragement and positive messages from his father and a sister, whom he indicated did not want to him end up "not doing well like she did":

DM: You've always been a good student?

T: I've never really struggled. In first and second grade, I never really did my homework because I wanted to be cool and I wanted to be like all the guys. My sister took me ice skating one time. Me and her just sat down and we talked about school. She didn't do very well in school and she didn't want me to end up not doing well like she did. Everybody thought [I] was smart. Her and my dad got me into hockey. Ever since I started playing hockey, my dad has been on my case to do my work. Keep my grades up in school. If I don't, that's the end of my hockey career. The most respect I get from anything is from hockey. . . . I want to be the best in hockey so I work hard in school to be able to play hockey.

....

DM: What are your favorite classes?

T: I like English because I like to write. I'm not much of a poem writer but I want to write poems. That's what I want to do. Nobody knows. I never told anybody that I want to write poems but that's what I want to do. So, I like English. My mentor is Langston Hughes. I look up to him.

Perception of Peers and School Climate

When talking about his peers, Terrell expressed the same sentiments as the other students I interviewed. He acknowledged that there were some good students at Hillside but that there were many more who did not do well. He attributed their inability to do well to a lack of will and determination. At the same time, he talked about his own personal resolve to resist the negative patterns:

DM: How would you describe this school? The kids, the teachers, the learning that goes on?

T: I'd say it has a bad reputation but the school is better than what people say it is. . . . We have a lot of A students at this school but we also have a lot of F students. It's more F students than there are A students. There's more D students also. There's no C students. You can actually pick out the A students. You can tell A students from F students.

....

DM: As far as you can tell, do you think a lot of the kids care about being successful or wanting to do well in school?

T: A lot of them care but it's just that a lot of them don't have that will to want to do it. The only way you can have a strong will is if you *want* to do this. You have to go to school [thinking] I want to do my work. I'm going to do it. It's gonna get done and if it doesn't get done, I'm going to take it home and I'm going to finish it. That's how I am.

DM: Do you think the kids see any long-term benefits to schooling?

T: Not really. It's few. A lot of them do it because they have to. Their parents. I do it because I want to. I want to succeed. A lot of kids do it because they have to. They don't want to work hard. They don't want to do their work. Very few of them do it because they want to.

Perceptions of Teachers

Although he did refer to problems with one of his teachers, Terrell had mostly positive perceptions of the teachers at Hillside and considered their efforts to be one of the elements that kept the school going. In Terrell's view there were some teachers who understood the difficulties students faced and believed they could succeed despite the unfortunate circumstances that may have defined their lives:

DM: When you look at this school, what would you say are the biggest strengths?

T: The biggest strength would have to be the teachers. Not every teacher is like what I'm about to explain but most teachers are. How can you have a kid coming from a broken home, poor, and no family giving him any type of push to work hard and have a teacher like Mrs. [Jones]. She recognizes in a minute how smart the kid can be and she'll encourage that kid. She knows the bad kids. She still tries hard with a lot of the kids she feels are bad kids. She still tries hard to get them to work. She'll encourage a kid to do their best all the time. No matter what kind of home that kid comes from. No matter what his will power is. No matter what his self-esteem. She'll encourage that kid to do his best. That's why I'm saying the teachers are the best strength here. Because of the way the teachers push the kids to do their best.

Beliefs About Differential Treatment

Of all the students interviewed in the study, Terrell expressed the strongest and most painful feelings about differential treatment from his peers. Not only did he believe that his peers put him down for his academic performance but also because he played hockey, which some of them regarded as a "White man's sport." During his interview, Terrell recalled the anguish he felt about this treatment and how he felt a sense of fear of returning to school each day. He was especially frustrated that he was being treated differently by other Black students:

DM: Do people around here, in the school, know about you [playing hockey]?

T: Everybody in the school knows about me but it's not like I get respect. Because people think of hockey as a White man's sport. But I think if a man wants to play hockey or a man wants to do something he wants to do, then he should be able to do it without anybody questioning how he does it or why he does it. I come to school everyday and [other kids say] "Terrell is a White boy. He talks proper. He plays hockey." But I live with that. That's just something I grew up with. . . . I always had it tough. I go home at night, every night, before I go to bed I think "Why do I get treated this way? Why can't I be good in school and also have a good social life?" Because nobody wants me to. I'm so much different from everybody. Everybody's different but I'm really different. Everything about me is different from everybody. . . . When I come out here. I [wonder if] I'm dressing right today because people are going to make fun of me. I'm self-conscious because I'm worried about how people are going to treat me. I don't particularly like being treated like I am. . . . I just live with it. What goes around comes around.

DM: Does that kind of pressure stop you from being successful and trying to stay on track or does it ever get in your way? What effect does it have on you?

T: People call me nerd because I do my work and I work hard in whatever I do. It distracts me because it hurts that my own race of people are putting me down. I might be one of the people that prevails among all people yet they don't want me to be successful. They might be successful out there doing bad things. I'm successful in class and I do my work. I'm successful in school and hockey but nobody gives me credit for it. I give myself credit and my dad gives me credit and my family. . . . It's a no-win situation. It's no way to win.

MELODY: "I DON'T WANT TO HAVE TO STRUGGLE"

Melody was a 14-year-old ninth-grader at the time of the interview. She lived with her mom and two sisters in Oakland. Her older sister was 16 years old and attended boarding school in a nearby county. Melody had also attended private school in her early grades. Her mother, who graduated from high school, is a teaching assistant at a small religious school in Oakland. The school was Muslim-based and this was also Melody's religion.

Melody is a very close friend of Paulette and they share many personal traits. But, unlike Paulette, Melody insisted that she had always maintained a separation between her personal goals and peer pressure to do otherwise. As a result, she has maintained mostly small friendship groups and has devoted significant attention to her studies. She maintained exemplary grade point averages throughout the year, was determined to succeed in life, and showed that a large part of her sense-of-self was tied to her academic achievement. She also displayed the same tendency as other students in this chapter to attribute much of her success to her own efforts and agency:

> DM: How would you describe yourself as a person?
>
> M: I think I take responsibility for [my actions]. My mom doesn't ask to see my report cards. If I wanted to, I could mess up. But she knows that most of the time I'm going to take responsibility for my actions. . . . I'm fun. I have a lot of associates but I only have a couple of friends. . . . I don't list everybody that I meet as my friend. . . . If they're like me and they have at least some goal in life. Sometimes, even when they don't have a goal, you can see something in them. Like they really care. Basically, if they're nice. If they're not trying to pull me down.
>
> DM: How would you describe yourself as a student?
>
> M: I'm not perfect. I'd say that I'm a student that gets my work done. I have to get my work done. I do good on my tests. A lot of times I don't even study. If I pay attention in class, most of the time I get it. I get along with most of my teachers. . . . When I first got here, I got 3.83 [grade point average], then I started getting 3.33. Then I got 3.50. This last report card period, I got a 3.83. For this last [marking period], I'm trying to get a 4.0.
>
> . . . .
>
> DM: Let's say all of sudden you started getting Fs. How would you feel?
>
> M: I would probably cry. . . . I don't know what I would I do.
>
> DM: Do you see that as a real possibility?
>
> M: No. . . . I want [a] career too bad.

Personal Goals and Motivation to Learn

When discussing the reasons for her success and why she had been able to stay on track in her coursework, Melody cited aspects of her strong personal identity and her internal disposition to succeed. Although she did receive encouragement from her mother, she took it on herself to do what she thought was necessary to succeed:

DM: Have you always been a good student in terms of your grades?

M: Yes. I would give part of the credit to me taking responsibility. . . . Me wanting the grades. . . . I feel that I have to do it on my own anyway.

DM: What about at home? Does your mom push you?

M: It's just me. . . . She helps me get into programs and then I'll do it for myself from then on.

....

DM: Do you have any role models?

M: Not as far as academics.

More than any other student, Melody was motivated by the need to achieve financial success. At several points in our interview, she mentioned her desire to make a lot of money and to be able to afford the things in life that she wanted. She seemed convinced that the only way to do this was to stay in school. She expressed a desire to be a doctor or an engineer and had taken the initiative to explore how these two interests might be combined:

DM: Have you always liked school?

M: I like school. I feel I have to go so I can make money. I don't want to be broke or homeless. I just feel that's the reason why I come here. . . . I want to make a lot of money. That's my main purpose. Also, I don't want to be stupid. I want to have a good career and make a lot of money. That's my main purpose for doing good.

DM: What do you want to do?

M: [The Mathematics, Engineering, and Science Association] got me interested in engineering. So for a long time I wanted to be a mechanical engineer. I took a mechanical engineering class. That was fun. But I always wanted to be a doctor, too. I talked to a lady at MESA and she said you could do both of them. There's a field called Biomedical Engineering. If I don't do that I think I want to be a pharmacist. They make a lot of money.

....

DM: How far do you want to go to school?

M: As far as I have to go to make the money.

Another factor that motivated Melody to succeed was rooted in her family experiences. At one time, her mother was working in a well-paying job and, for personal reasons, decided to give it up. As a result, the family's standard of living fell. Melody expressed a great deal of frustration and disappointment about this decision and maintained a strong resolve to avoid having to struggle like her mother. The message inherent in her mother's struggle had a powerful effect on Melody's drive, determination, and commitment to success and made her place a great deal of emphasis on the instrumental value of her education:

DM: Is that one of the biggest reasons for you [to think math is important], to get a good job?

M: Uh huh. I don't want to struggle for nothing if I don't have to. I want to live a decent life. I don't want to be rich or anything. I want to be able to provide for my kids if I have to. I don't want us to have to struggle month by month.

DM: Do you see other people that have to go through that struggle? Where are you getting that image from?

M: From myself, my own family. I [say to myself] I do not want to be like this when I grow up. My mom had a good job. . . She decided to quit. She had a good job and we were doing good. I was [thinking] why did she do that?

DM: It seems like that's kind of a motivation for you to do well?

M: Yeah, it's true.

DM: Is it motivation to do better or just to do different?

M: To do different and better.

DM: Does your mom know about the way you think?

M: Yes. I tell her, I'm not going to be like you. . . . She's a good
        mom. She provides for us in every way she can. . . . But I
        don't want to have to struggle.

DM: Do you really think school is going to make a difference in
        changing the long-term for you?

M: Uh huh. . . . It's not like how it was for my mom getting a
        good job with a high school diploma. Now you got to have
        computer skills, graduate school, internships.

Perceptions of Peers and School Climate

Melody was also very eager to differentiate and distance herself from
most of the students at Hillside. She, too, recognized that there were
two main student cultures at Hillside: a small group of high-achievers
and a much larger group whose attitudes and behaviors she suggested
indicated that they did not want to succeed and did not care about
school:

DM: Do you like this school?

M: Not really. I wouldn't recommend it to nobody. If you come
        here a lot of people think that you don't learn nothing. But
        if you want to learn, you can learn. . . . But as far as how
        organized they are and how friendly they are, no. . . . A lot
        of the kids are rowdy. Some of them [are here] to learn. The
        majority of the kids are up here for play. Just to pass the
        time. . . . Most of them walk the halls. In the bathrooms.
        Loud. Not acting how they should. A lot of them are just
        following the crowd.

DM: How can you tell the kids who are doing what they are
        supposed to be doing?

M: Because I see them in the awards assembly. I see them in
        the honor roll. I can kind of tell.

In contrast to her peers, Melody was forward-thinking and took
advantage of the opportunities that were available at Hillside. She
also maintained a strong sense of individuality and defined herself in
opposition to the traits that she ascribed to her peers:

DM: You mentioned a couple of times that you feel it falls on
       you, that it's your responsibility [to do well]. You also
       mentioned that sometimes other kids do different things.
       Do you let that stuff get in your way?

M: No. Not really. . . . A lot of the students, how they act. I
       wouldn't want to act like that. That's my motto—to not act
       how they act. . . . I don't feel I need to fit in. I'm not trying
       to fit in. . . . I see the long-term. . . . They don't care about
       the long-term.

Perceptions of Teachers

Although very critical of her peers, Melody made positive comments
about her teachers and cited their ability to withstand the rigors of
teaching at Hillside:

DM: What would you say is the biggest strength of the school
       and what's the thing that's kind of taking it down?

M: The biggest strength is the faculty. They put up with all of
       it. . . . What's pulling it down is that the [administration is]
       not organized.

Mathematics Identity: Beliefs
About Mathematical Ability

Melody expressed a high level of confidence about her mathematics
ability and justifiably believed that she was one of the better math
students at Hillside. Melody also received recognition for her
mathematical abilities by being selected to participate in the
Mathematics, Engineering, and Science Association, an enrichment
program sponsored by the University of California:

DM: How is your math class going? You're taking geometry?
       How is that class going for you?

M: It's going good. I like it. . . . I started out as a B. Then I got a
       B+. From now on, I've been getting As.

DM: Do you like math?

M: Yes, I've always liked math.

DM: Are you good at math?

M: I feel I'm doing pretty good.

DM: Where would you put yourself? Are you in the top, the middle, the bottom?

M: In the school, I would say I was at the top. For my geometry class, I would say everybody is about on the same level.

Mathematics Identity: Beliefs About Importance of Mathematics

Because she had firm beliefs about the role of education in helping her to reach her goals, it was not surprising that Melody assigned high instrumental value to mathematics. Not only was she receptive to the positive messages she received from others about mathematics but she bought into the idea enough that she did not want to "risk" not taking it:

DM: Do you see any reasons to keep taking math classes?

M: Yeah, I see a reason. It gets you into college. If you don't know it, you aren't going to be able to get a good job like computers or something. So, I feel I have to take it.

DM: Since you want to go into engineering you can see how math is involved. Did somebody have to tell you that or is it something that you began to see the connections for yourself?

M: I heard it a lot. But then I started seeing it for myself.

DM: Is math important to you?

M: It's important. Because everybody talks about math. [They say] you need math, you need math. So, I'm not going to risk it. I might as well take it.

JASMINE: "YOU CANNOT GO ANYWHERE OR DO ANYTHING IN THE WORLD WITHOUT USING MATH"

Jasmine was a twelve-year-old seventh-grader who lived with her parents, a younger brother, and a younger sister at the time of the interview. Her father is a computer engineer for IBM who attended a prestigious, predominately African-American university on the east coast. Her mother, who works for a bottled water company, did not attend college.

I observed Jasmine on a daily basis in Mrs. Allgood's fourth period and considered her to be among the most gifted seventh-grade students at Hillside. However, she often seemed bored and frustrated by what she considered the slow pace necessary to teach her peers. Because of this, she often talked out of turn and acted out in other ways that displayed her growing frustration. She criticized the classroom activities as too easy and boring and criticized Mrs. Allgood for not giving out work that was challenging.

Personal Identity

Jasmine displayed an extremely strong personal identity and sense-of-self. She knew that she was smart and was very confident about her abilities. Jasmine was also aware of the negative influences, like peer pressure, that surrounded her at Hillside. But she was able to invoke a strong sense of personal agency and resist these forces:

DM: How would you describe yourself as a person?

J: Able to express my opinion when wanting to. I'm nice. Not shy. Outgoing, I don't let peer pressure get to me, I'm my own person and nobody can tell me what to do or when to do it or why to do it.

DM: Who taught you that or why do you believe that?

J: My parents and me. Because I have seen cases where people do something because their friend does it.

DM: You don't believe in that kind of thing?

J: Um um.

Personal Goals and Motivation to Learn

Jasmine expressed several reasons for wanting to do well in school and succeed in life. In addition to her own personal resolve, she was also motivated by her parents' expectations. Although I did not ask her about her African-American identity or whether she believed that her life would be more difficult because she was Black, Jasmine did tell me that she was also motivated by a desire to break racial stereotypes about African-Americans. In particular, she indicated a desire to attend Harvard University to show people that an African-American could do so:

DM: Does anybody at home encourage you to do good?

J: My father and my mother.

DM: What do they say?

J: Only do things to your best advantage.

DM: What about help with your schoolwork?

J: Yeah. They help with my homework.

....

DM: What if you got all F's?

J: I would get in trouble. Both of my parents. . . . They'll take away a privilege.

....

DM: How far do you want to go in school?

J: I'm going to go to either Howard [University] or Harvard.

DM: Why do you want to go to those schools?

J: I want to go to Howard because my father went to that school and that is a good school. I want to go to Harvard because I want to achieve something and they wouldn't expect a Black person to be at Harvard.

Perceptions of Peers and School Climate

Jasmine was very critical of the behaviors and attitudes of her peers. During the entire year of the study, she maintained friendships with only a small number of other female students and did not interact much with other students:

DM: How would you describe the students?

J: It depends on what kind of students you're talking about. My friends are good. I don't hang around people that I know will get me into trouble. So I hang around people that will have a positive effect on me.

DM: What about other kids?

J: Well, they're bad. They like getting in trouble. They don't care about themselves or others. They think getting in trouble makes you look better. . . . I think some of them are at their level. . . . I don't even think they're learning. The way they be acting, I don't even think they're learning. I think it goes in one ear and out the other. . . . Some don't come to class. Some just sit there and fall asleep. Some don't ever turn in work. Some talk back to Mrs. Allgood. . . . It seems that they don't like math. I know they know how important it is, they just don't really care.

Perceptions of Teachers

Jasmine was also critical of the administration and teachers, characterizing them as unable to formulate programs and plans for students who were doing well such as herself:

DM: Do you like school this year?

J: Some parts of school have been very, very bad. . . . The organization of the school such as the GATE [Gifted and Talented Education Program]. So far this school year, nothing has been done for the students that are in that program. So they aren't learning anything. Especially if they already know the stuff they're learning. The school is so unorganized that it hasn't done anything yet.

Mathematics Identity: Beliefs About Mathematical Ability

Jasmine was very confident in her mathematical ability but also expressed a concern that she was not learning enough. She characterized many of the topics covered in her class as too easy. Early in the year, she became disinterested and did not put forth her best effort in her math class. As a result, Mrs. Allgood gave her a C. After facing the consequences from her parents, she increased her effort despite her boredom with the class:

DM: How is math class going for you?

J: Honestly, it's boring. . . . I know all that stuff she is teaching and I don't feel that I should learn stuff that I already know. If you're on a higher level than other kids, I think that should be acknowledged. . . . First marking period, I wasn't involved because I realized that I knew the stuff and I just let go and didn't do anything and I got a C.

DM: You weren't really interested because you already knew it? What made you change?

J: That grade. . . . I knew I could get better than that. I just wasn't trying.

....

DM: What did your parents say when you got a C?

J: They put me on punishment. Because my father expects a lot out of me and he says I should never get lower than a B.

....

DM: Are you good at math?

J: Yeah . . . I am. I just know it.

DM: Do you have a lot of confidence in your ability?

J: Yeah. I think I'm at the top of the class.

DM: Do you think the other kids think you're good at math?

J: Yeah. They're always asking me for help and stuff.

Mathematics Identity: Beliefs
About the Importance of Math

Despite her boredom in class, Jasmine did consider mathematics as being important. She also indicated that her reasons for learning it extended beyond her liking or not liking it. She saw it as important to get a job and to function in day-to-day life:

DM: Do you like math?

J: It's not a question of if I like it. I gotta survive with it, so I gotta stick with it.

DM: What do you mean you gotta stick with it?

J: Jobs. You cannot go anywhere or do anything in the world without using math.

DM: Who told you that?

J: Me. It's obvious.

DM: What career do you want?

J: I want to be a corporate lawyer.

DM: Do you think you'll need math for that?

J: I don't think, I know I need math for that.

Beliefs About Differential Treatment

Jasmine, like her peers in this chapter, cited differential treatment from her peers as one of the prices she paid for her success. Like the other students, Jasmine did not let the actions of other students stand in her way. She continued to maintain her beliefs in her ability and her goals:

DM: The fact that you're a good student, how do other students treat you?

J: They call me a nerd. Because nerds are smart and do all their work. . . . Sticks and stones may break my bones but words will never hurt me. . . . I'm my own person and I'm not going to change because they call me names. If I'm a nerd then I'm just a nerd. They call me a nerd because they're jealous that they ain't as smart as I am. Not meaning to say I'm conceited or nothing. I'm proud of it.

CARL: "I DOUBT IF ANYONE MAKES IT IN LIFE WITHOUT MATH"

Carl was a 12-year-old seventh-grader at the time of this interview. He lived with his parents in Oakland. His mother completed college and his father completed 2 years of college. His mother is a school teacher in the Oakland Unified School District and his father is a truck driver. He has one older brother and two older sisters. One of his sisters attended high school and the other was a student at a California State University. Carl played basketball for the seventh-grade team and was in the school band, playing both the saxophone and the clarinet. Carl described himself as quiet. He had a very serious demeanor and had very strong opinions about the other students at Hillside. He also had very strong opinions about the importance of education:

DM: Do you like school this year?

C: I like it a lot. It's different things.

DM: Have you always liked school?

C: Always! I dislike being out. Summer is okay but I don't like being out on teachers' break. I just don't like it. I don't know why. . . . Sometimes if I'm sick or if my head is hurting or something and my mother is telling me to stay home, I don't want to stay home.

Personal Goals and Motivation to Learn

Carl was motivated to learn partly because of his belief in the instrumental value of education. He believed that without education, his life would meet with unfortunate circumstances:

DM: Why do you stay on track? Why do you want to keep doing well?

C: You got to have your education. If you don't have your education and I [go for a job] and don't have an education on my records... they'll say you never finished school and can't give you a job if you don't have a full education. . . . I don't want to end up on the streets.

      . . . .

DM: If you got all Fs, how would that make you feel?

C: That would make me feel down. But it wouldn't mean nothing to me if I did it [on purpose]. If I came to class with no books, chewing gum, didn't care. I probably wouldn't care. Why are you going to care if you do it on purpose?

Perceptions of School Climate and Peers

Carl's comments about his peers at Hillside were similar to those of the other students in this chapter. He believed that Hillside was a good school and could be a good place to learn except for behavior of some of the students:

DM: How would you describe this school. If somebody didn't know about it?

C: I would describe it as good. Should be better. A lot better. The teachers are okay. They teach good. The children, I think they need better behavior. . . . That's one big, major issue. That's one reason why Hillside has so bad of a name. They say kids' basic grade-point-average is not over a 2.0. At least get a 2.0, I would think. If you don't have a 2.0 and you're not going to class, you might as well not come to school.

DM: Is a lot of the students like that or is just some?

C: It's a good percentage.

DM: What about the ones that don't act like that? Why do you think they don't do all that stuff?

C: They rather do education and they want to have a healthy life.

Perceptions of Teachers

Carl had mostly positive comments about his teachers but was also critical of those he considered to be mean:

DM: What do you think your teachers think about you?

C: They probably think of me as a young man who is intelligent who does his work.

DM: The teachers. Anything else you have to say about them?

C: They're good. Some of them are kind of mean, but not all of them. They grade you the way you are in class [based on] the way you do your work and stuff. They're good.

Mathematics Identity: Beliefs
About Mathematical Ability

Although he received fairly good grades in mathematics and was an active participant in his math class, Carl was somewhat modest about his ability. Because of his grades, he considered himself to be average. In addition to his modesty, Carl also felt that he needed to succeed by his own efforts—that asking for help somehow highlighted weakness on his part. Despite these feelings, he was one of the better students in his class:

DM: What about your math class? How is that class going?

C: Mrs. Allgood. She teaches good.

....

DM: Are you satisfied with how you're doing or do you think you should be doing better?

C: I think I should be doing better. . . . Most of the time, I've gotten a C. I think I should have at least a B+ or an A-. Math is one of the easiest subjects. . . . I've always liked math. When I was in first grade. . . . I had left everybody in the first-grade math book and I was in the second-grade math book.

DM: Where would you put yourself, in the top, the middle or the bottom of the class?

C: At least the middle. . . . Because I feel that more people can do math better than I can. I feel that I slouched after sixth grade. I wasn't doing it good. . . . I got a B [in math] last time.

....

DM: If you have trouble in class, what do you usually do?

C: Sometimes, I ask one of my friends but sometimes I don't want to ask them. I feel that it's the world versus me in it and I don't have no help. In college, you're not going to have help. The teachers give you the work and they don't say the answer is so and so.

DM: So do you feel shy about asking for help?

C: No, not really. I'll ask for help but I feel that I should learn it on my own. If I know that I know something and I'm asking for help, I feel that's the wrong thing for me to do.

Mathematics Identity: Beliefs About the Importance of Mathematics

Although Carl did not have a very sophisticated view of the instrumental importance of mathematics, he did recognize some of its practical uses and thought that math was essential to function in life:

DM: Do you see any reasons for having to learn math? Are you going to need it for anything? What's the use of it?

C: I think you need to learn math. A lot. Let's say they never taught math and you go into a grocery store and you do a subtotal yourself. If you don't know math, how are you going to say that $100 + 20 = 120$?

....

DM: Is math important to you or is it just another subject?

C: It's important.

DM: Did somebody tell you that or is that something you believe?

C: That's something I think. I doubt if anybody makes it in life without math.

DISCUSSION

Prior studies of mathematics achievement and persistence among Black students have focused primarily on failure, offering several explanations for this failure. The case studies I've presented contrast sharply with these typical portrayals. They show that African-American students can achieve success in mathematics, whether as a pursuit in itself or within the context of their larger academic efforts. Moreover, they do so in light of and in spite of school and community forces. Although these students faced many of the in-school and out-of-school conditions that are often thought of as preventing them from succeeding, they did succeed. These students demonstrated determination and resilience in the face of negative forces, and intelligence and wisdom in the context of positive forces.

What many prior studies have failed to explain is why some students, who must face sometimes tough community and school forces manage to succeed when many of their peers do not. In particular, few studies have examined individual student agency in ways that explain how students transform and internalize their experiences and respond productively to the forces they encounter. As the data in this chapter have shown, a number of factors contributed to academic and mathematics success among the students profiled, including the strength of their personal and mathematics identities. Table 4.2 briefly summarizes the beliefs and identities of each student in terms of the themes listed in Table 4.1.

Personal Identities and Goals.

Successful students possessed very strong senses of personal identity and engaged in positive self-definition. This was not true for many of their peers who appeared to seek the approval of other peers and behaved in ways that allowed them to fit in. Successful students were motivated to succeed and were beginning to establish particular short-term and long-term goals for success even if they could not fully articulate them. They were cognizant of their success and were well aware of the requirements necessary to maintain it. They often referred to their peers as the antithesis of who they wanted to be and maintained a resolve not to let their peers deter them from reaching their goals. These students' motivations were also fueled by personal experiences outside of school. They recognized the consequences of not succeeding or doing well in their studies, such as ending up on welfare, or dropping out of school, or not getting a good job.

Perceptions of School Climate and Peers.

Among successful students, there was a consistent perception that a majority of their peers were underachievers and did not take full advantage of the opportunities available to them in school. These students often commented on the negative aspects of their school atmosphere and pointed out how these factors disrupted their studies as well as to teachers' ability to reach students who did want to learn. They readily identified groups of students whom they considered "the bad kids" and those whom considered "the nerds" or "good kids."

TABLE 4.2
Key Themes for Student Success

	Lisa	*Paulette*	*Annette*	*Terrell*	*Melody*	*Jasmine*	*Carl*
Personal identities and goals	Positive	Positive	Positive	Positive	Positive	Positive	Positive
Perceptions of peers	Critical	Critical	Critical	Critical	Critical	Critical	Critical
Perception	Positive	Positive Critical	Positive Critical	Positive Critical	Neutral	Positive Critical	Positive Critical
Beliefs about mathematical ability	Positive	Positive	Positive	Positive	Positive	Positive	Mixed
Motivation to obtain mathematical knowledge	High	High	High	High	High	High	High
Valued instrumental importance of mathematical knowledge?	Yes	Yes	Yes	Yes	Yes	Yes	Yes
Experienced Differential treatment from peers?	Yes	Yes	Yes	Yes	Yes	Yes	Yes

They consistently placed themselves in the "good kids" group and did not care about negative labels that their peers tried to assign them. Some, but not all, indicated that they did not consider their school a "safe" place, given the possibility of being attacked by jealous peers or by someone who just wanted to start trouble. As a result, many of them maintained small friendship groups and devoted most of their attention to academic pursuits and school sanctioned social events.

Perceptions of Teachers.

Unlike many of the students who did not seem to get along with teachers, most of the successful students indicated a high level of respect and appreciation for the efforts of the teachers. Although they were critical of some classroom activities, they maintained a consistent belief that teachers were interested in teaching and were helpful if asked. This was in stark contrast to many of the less successful students observed in this study. Many of them frequently complained about teachers and often engaged in disrespectful or disruptive behaviors in their teacher's presence.

Beliefs About Differential Treatment.

Despite their success and positive self images, several of the successful students identified various forms of differential treatment that they faced from their peers. This treatment ranged from good-natured teasing and being called "nerd" to accusations of trying to "act White." Despite this teasing, most maintained a strong resolve to continue in the pursuit of their goals and not let the actions of others deter them from their goals. (The one exception might be Terrell, whose experiences with differential treatment were severe enough to cause him a great deal of personal anguish.) They were very forward-thinking and believed that later in life, they would reap the benefits of their hard work.

Mathematics Identity
Among Successful Students

Given their strong personal identities as well the influence of parents, teachers, and peers, most of the successful students were able to utilize their experiences with these significant others to develop positive mathematics identities. These identities were reflected in their beliefs about their math abilities, their motivation to learn mathematics, and their beliefs about its instrumental importance.

Beliefs About Mathematics Ability and Motivation to Learn.

A majority of the successful students interviewed expressed a strong belief in their mathematics ability and a high level of motivation to achieve mathematics success. Most students felt that they were among the best in their class and were disappointed when they received low grades. Most expressed concern over getting Bs or lower. Surprisingly, some of the students, despite their success, expressed modestly low levels of confidence about their abilities and placed themselves "in the middle" of the class. Many of these students (Lisa, Sheneka, Annette, Melody) identified math class as one of their favorites despite not liking particular activities or particular aspects of the classroom practices and activities. Even in those cases where math was not identified as a favorite class, students still attempted to maintain their grades and complete their work, indicating they at least recognized the importance of doing well.

Beliefs About the Instrumental Importance of Mathematics.

All of the students profiled in this chapter contextualized the importance of mathematics and mathematics knowledge in either socioeconomic terms (i.e., necessary to get a "good" job) or as a prerequisite to the steps leading to a promising future (i.e., necessary to get into college). Although few students could identify people from their communities who had actually achieved success based on knowledge of mathematics, they all seemed to share beliefs about its importance. Their levels of knowledge about the instrumental importance of mathematics learning ranged from the very simple ("being able to count my money"), to the those with limited awareness—"to take college tests and be ready for college courses," to some awareness of possible economic rewards ("I want to be a teacher and I might decide to teach math or I might want to be a doctor and I need to know a lot of math and science").

The student narratives in this chapter help shed light on mathematics success among African-American students. We saw that important factors fueling their success were their abilities to think about school and mathematics learning in broader contexts, to develop goals that take advantage of this knowledge, and to invoke the kind of individual agency that was necessary to help them achieve their goals.

5

Mathematics Socialization and Identity Among African-Americans:

Real Life Experiences, Research, and Recommendations

I opened this book with a discussion of the personal and professional experiences that helped motivate me to search for compelling explanations of mathematics achievement and persistence among African-Americans. I described a plan of research that would eventually take me to mathematics classrooms at Hillside Junior High School. There, I found students and teachers who were engaged in an ongoing struggle to implement and adjust to significant changes in their mathematics curriculum.

As a result of my early and unanticipated discovery of these difficulties, my initial, more narrowly focused concerns with math content and curricular practices soon expanded to include issues of community forces and community beliefs about mathematics. This expanded focus was necessary because the beliefs and practices that I observed among teachers and students at Hillside could not be explained by content and curricular issues alone. This realization, in turn, led me to the homes of African-American parents and community members, where I explored their personal and collective histories and the natures of their mathematical experiences.

What I learned from my interviews and observations of students, teachers, parents, and community members about their mathematics socializations and identities served to support three claims made throughout this book:

- Mathematics learning, achievement, and persistence among African-Americans must be examined within their broader contexts—sociohistorical, socioeconomic, community, family, school, classroom, curricular, and peer group.

- The experiences that characterize mathematics socialization and affect mathematics identity among African-Americans provide an important interpretive framework with which to understand outcomes in mathematics achievement and persistence.

- African-American parents and adolescents are not passive in their mathematics socializations but exhibit a wide range of agency-related behaviors that affect their success or failure.

My analyses in chapters 2, 3, and 4 showed that schools are just one of many contexts in which African-Americans receive mixed messages about the importance of mathematics. The analyses in those chapters showed that the messages generated within these contexts can be very powerful and can profoundly influence one's mathematics identity.

Just as important, my arguments demonstrate that although sociohistorical, community, and school forces had powerful effects on the mathematics socializations and identities of the participants in my study, the participants were not passive recipients of these experiences. They were able to exercise a great deal of agency in the face of such forces—actively constructing meanings for mathematics learning and mathematics knowledge and acting on those meanings accordingly. For example, some parents, like Sarah and Wendy, were able to overcome early, negative mathematics experiences, reinvest in mathematics learning, and construct goals and expectations that reflected a recognition of the instrumental importance of mathematics—if not for themselves, then for their children.

In addition, students at Hillside invoked their agency in two dramatically different ways: successful students by resisting the achievement and behavioral norms that prevailed in their peer groups, and unsuccessful students by resisting many of the practices stressed in their mathematics classrooms and perpetuating the strong norm of underachievement that existed among a majority of students. This student agency highlights the fact that schools and classrooms—the contexts that attract the most attention from mathematics educators—are more than arenas of reproduction and oppression.

In the remainder of this chapter, I continue to discuss my arguments about mathematics socialization and identity, both in terms of what they say about why mathematics learning and teaching unfolded in the ways it did at Hillside and also in terms of what these very local results say about broader issues in mathematics learning and persistence among African-Americans.

I conclude by highlighting the contributions and implications of my research for mathematics educators, African-American parents and community members, African-American students, and teachers of African-American students.

Perhaps the best way to flesh out the final part of my discussion is to revisit a number of issues raised at the beginning of this book and review them in retrospect. This strategy will also help to further map out the key components of my theoretical perspective and framework and highlight relationships between those themes I identified as being particularly important in mathematics socialization and identity. Those themes, first introduced in chapter 1, are reproduced in Table 5.1.

HOW DID THEIR SOCIOECONOMIC AND EDUCATIONAL EXPERIENCES CHARACTERIZE MATHEMATICS SOCIALIZATION AND AFFECT IDENTITY AMONG AFRICAN-AMERICAN PARENTS AND COMMUNITY MEMBERS?

The largest contexts that I consider in my analysis of mathematics identity and socialization consisted of sociohistorical and community forces. Sociohistorical forces were highlighted in chapter 1 where I briefly discussed the persistent discrimination and differential treatment that many African-Americans have faced in societal, socioeconomic, and educational contexts. It has been well documented that these historical practices partially account for the evolution of certain cultural and occupational roles, and I believe they also help explain long-standing underrepresentation in areas like mathematics. In particular, we know that slightly more than 30 years ago, these practices prevented African-Americans from entering into mathematics-related arenas and even linger today to affect their beliefs and perceptions about opportunities and constraints they face.

To see how these historical forces manifested themselves in the day-to-day lives of African-American parents and community members in this study, I investigated what I called *community beliefs about mathematics*. I did this by considering aspects of the individual life

TABLE 5.1
Multilevel Framework for Analyzing
Mathematics Socialization and Identity Among African-Americans:
Key Themes

Sociohistorical

Differential treatment in mathematics-related contexts

Community

- Beliefs about African-American status and differential treatment in educational and socioeconomic contexts

- Beliefs about mathematics abilities and motivation to learn mathematics

- Beliefs about the instrumental importance of mathematics knowledge

- Relationships with school officials and teachers

- Math-dependent socioeconomic and educational goals

- Expectations for children and educational strategies

School

- Institutional agency and school-based support systems

- Teachers' curricular goals and content decisions

- Teachers' beliefs about student abilities and motivation to learn

- Teachers' beliefs about African-American parents and communities

- Student culture and achievement norms

- Classroom negotiation of mathematical and social norms

Agency and Mathematics Success
Among African-American Students

- Personal identities and goals

- Perceptions of school climate, peers, and teachers

- Beliefs about mathematics abilities and motivation to learn

- Beliefs about the instrumental importance of mathematics knowledge

- Beliefs about differential treatment from peers

---

histories as well as the shared, collective experiences of African-American parents and community members in those larger socioeconomic and educational contexts where mathematics played an important role.

What I found surprising was the degree to which parents and community members were able to narrow their wide-ranging discussions about their general life experiences to the area of mathematics learning—providing clear evidence of important parallels and relationships between the developments of their African-American identities and their mathematics identities.

Equally surprising was the degree to which their early mathematics experiences affected the overall senses-of-self among parents and community members. But this occurred in different ways—in some cases having a negative, detrimental affect and in other cases serving as strong motivation to overcome prior negative experiences. This finding points out that African-Americans do not have uniform responses to their experiences.

For example, we saw that Tina's feelings about being a helpful mother were closely tied to her feelings about her limited mathematics ability and subsequent inability to help her children:

> It really frustrates me when [my children] come to me and they say, "Mom, we have math and we can't do this and we can't do that." [I have to tell them] "But mom doesn't know how to do it either." So, I have to stop and I have to think sometimes. "I guess I can help you. I guess I can try." . . . When they have their own children and one comes to them, they won't have to say "Oh, well, momma can't help you with this because I don't know how." They'll be able to say "Come on, let's sit down and I'll help you." If it's math, English, whatever, they'll have no problem with helping their own children.

Wendy made similar comments but, unlike Tina, she was more determined to reinvest in mathematics for the sake of her children. After being unable to help her two oldest daughters, Wendy expressed a strong desire to be able to help the youngest. She also revealed, like Tina, that a part of her identity as a mother was closely linked to her beliefs about her mathematics abilities:

> I see math as important now because of my daughter. My oldest one is in math analysis and I wasn't able to help her at all. Once she got to algebra, I was like, "You're on your own." So, she had to learn it on her own. My middle daughter, she's in algebra now and she's on her own. I find it important because I have to help my children. Especially my baby because she's going into that. So, it's real important now. . . . I don't want her to be like her mom.

Finally, we saw that Sarah echoed the comments of both Tina and Wendy but her new-found success in mathematics had a very positive effect on her overall sense-of-self:

> I feel differently about [math] altogether because I'm learning it. One other thing that I felt good about was when my daughter was doing some exponents and she was sitting there and I was like "What ya doing?" and she says "Exponents." When I came over and explained it to her, I felt so good about it. It was like "I know this, I can show her. She'll get it right." I felt good about it. It gave me a different look on the situation. It was like "Oh. This *is* what I need to be doing."

I found these kind of comments surprising because there were, in the initial stages of this research, serious questions concerning my assumptions about the primacy of mathematics in the lives of the participants. In the bigger scheme of their life circumstances, why would or why should their mathematical experiences stand out in any particular way? Once I began my interviews, however, I soon discovered that parents' and community members' discussions of their mathematics experiences became important indicators of the kinds of experiences they had in other aspects of their lives. It also became apparent that those other experiences affected the nature of their mathematical experiences as well.

In addition to their effect on the participants' larger senses-of-self, I also found that the nature and quality of these mathematical experiences had a profound influence on how African-American parents and community members regarded mathematics, in terms of its instrumental importance and value as a school subject, their beliefs about their mathematics abilities, and their motivation to pursue mathematical knowledge.

For example, readers may recall that in talking about her early mathematical experiences Wendy remarked that somewhere along the line she "got lost" in mathematics and from that point on she never believed that she could succeed. These feelings about her ability did not change over the years even though she had recently experienced short-term success in her mathematics course at a local community college.

Wendy's inability to fully recover from her experiences could also be attributed to her long-standing beliefs and feelings about her White teachers, whom she believed were "not concerned about us " and who demonstrated this by "[setting] us over in the corner and would not let us learn."

Wendy's experiences were certainly not unique. When I interviewed Tina, she recalled similar experiences and had her own story to tell about her early mathematics socialization. Asked to comment on what caused her to value mathematics in the way that she did, Tina's response in chapter 2 was as follows:

[My teacher] didn't make it seem that important. To me, it was just another class. It was because that's the way he made us think. He made us think that math was not important. . . . Most of the students would say, "I don't care. It don't make me no difference." So, I would tell him and I would let him know I didn't care. "Fine, you want to give me an F. You want to fail me. Do it. I don't care. Because I don't see why we're here anyway." But that's just the way he made me feel. . . . He didn't come at me making me think that math is what I needed. Math is what I should have. Math should be a very important part of my life.

Finally, in Harold's case, these early mathematics experiences were not confined to school contexts but also extended to socioeconomic contexts. These experiences were characterized by stinging racism, discrimination, and explicit messages about limited opportunity. When asked to interpret these early life experiences, Harold made the following comments:

Well, most of [those barriers] were racially motivated. I could see that. . . . To have to be preoccupied with that reality I'm sure had something to do with one's desire to be an achiever. "Going for the gold," you might say. If you can't have it, why struggle for it. The whole culture at that time, it was an intimidating kind of culture that challenged an individual not to go beyond certain boundaries because there wasn't anything there for you.

Later in his interview, we learned that these experiences did, in fact, affect Harold's mathematics identity, especially his motivation to obtain mathematics knowledge, causing him to admit, sadly, that he "wasn't going to be doing any math."

I believe that their socioeconomic and educational experiences constitute a large part of the mathematics socialization process for African-American parents and community members. The analyses and findings presented in chapter 2 showed that the degree to which these early experiences were internalized had a dramatic affect not only on African-American parents' and community members' mathematics identities but also on the expectations and goals they set for their children. These expectations depended largely on the degree to which the parents, themselves, had recovered from their own early mathematics socializations. This was a clear indication that community beliefs about mathematics can be very powerful influences in the mathematical development of African-American children.

For example, although Sarah recalled placing little importance on mathematics learning and knowledge during her own youth, her reinvestment in mathematics learning and recent success, together with her hope of benefiting from such knowledge, caused her to develop high expectations for her children. She then acted on those expectations by becoming a strong advocate for her children. Partly because of these high expectations and positive agency, Sarah's two children were, in fact, doing above average school work. These more positive responses to their mathematical experiences highlight the kind of agency and investment that I believe African-American parents must demonstrate, despite their own negative mathematics experiences.

In contrast, my interviews with Harold and Tina showed that they never fully recovered from the negative experiences that seemed to characterize much of their mathematics socializations. In particular, Tina appeared to give up all hope of ever learning or benefiting from mathematics knowledge. For Harold, the effects of his experiences with racism and discrimination still lingered to the point that he believed, even in today's society, there was little opportunity for his son to benefit from obtaining mathematical knowledge. Unfortunately, both Harold and Tina expressed little in the way of high academic expectations for their children. As it turned out, none of their children were doing well in school.

My findings about these expressions of their expectations for their children also lend support to one of the methodological claims made in chapter 1. Rather than relying solely on traditional measures of mathematics attitude such as surveys—which tend to elicit responses reflecting mainstream, folk beliefs about the importance of mathematics, and which have lead to paradoxes and inconsistencies between stated beliefs and actual achievement—more informative data might be collected utilizing methods that link the mathematics experiences of African-American parents and community members to other areas of their lives.

These methods, such as ethnographic interviews, should address the kinds of experiences and messages parents receive about constraints and opportunities to benefit from mathematics; the kinds of mathematics identities that they develop; and whether they realistically expect their children to benefit from learning mathematics, encourage them to do so, and take the necessary action to make this possible.

Why Are Community Forces Important?

I strongly support the position of scholars inside and outside of mathematics education who emphasize the fact that schools are embedded in communities and, just as formal policies regarding pedagogy, curriculum, student sorting, and distribution of resources make their way into the school to affect teaching and learning, so do community forces.

For me, one of the most fruitful aspects of studying these community beliefs about mathematics is showing that the legacy of denied opportunity and differential treatment in mathematics contexts is a potent and viable factor that operates to inform and affect the day-to-day lives of many African-American adults. Their knowledge of and responses to this legacy influences their perceptions of themselves, their beliefs about their capabilities as parents, and their expectations for their children. I believe it is important that mathematics educators continue to try and understand the natures and effects of these experiences as well as the subsequent responses of African-American parents and community members. These community beliefs about mathematics contribute to the contexts that students look to for messages about the importance of mathematics and may represent the most important link in building sufficiently complex explanations for mathematics achievement and persistence among Black students.

Support for this focus comes from the fact that all of the parents profiled in chapter 2 and all but one of those interviewed but not profiled, listed these community beliefs about mathematics as a major factor affecting achievement and persistence among African-American students. Readers may recall the following comments made by Wendy, Tina, Sarah, and Harold when asked to explain limited presence by African-Americans in mathematical contexts as well as limited persistence and achievement by students:

Wendy: I don't think the parents put emphasis on it enough. It's with the parents. I don't know for sure but I don't think if I had stressed math [for my children], the counselors or the teachers wouldn't have did it. So, I think it's the parents that have to stress the importance. . . . I think the parents know [it's important]. I think they know, but a lot of parents are just so into letting a child be a child instead of preparing them for their future that they don't push it as hard. I think that they know that their child should take more than algebra but a lot of parents say, "Well, the counselor said this and the counselor said that and my teacher said this." I don't think that they realize that counselor or that teacher is White and they're not that concerned about your Black child as you should be.

Tina: There's nothing wrong with these kids' mathematics. These kids know the math, they know the work. They don't want to do it. . . . It hasn't been pushed on to them. It hasn't been said "This is what we feel that you should do in school."

Sarah: Because, like I said, I don't think they think it matters. It's like, "Why do I have to take this math class? I'm not going to use it." I don't they think it really matters. But it does. I see now that it does. But then I didn't think it really mattered. I think they get the attitude "I don't want to do this." So, they do it to get a grade and that's it. I believe that's why because they don't think it matters. They don't think they're going to use it later in life.

Harold: I think that might be true because of the fact that there's no incentives out there to excel in that area. We don't have no industry out there and the industry that is out there, they're not targeting the Black community and saying, "If you go and get more math, then I can guarantee you this." But the average Caucasian may know that with math . . . he knows where his market is for what he's going to get. The average Black American doesn't know what markets there are out there for math. They're not looking at [the fact that] NASA needs mathematicians. They're not looking at who needs skilled people at math. They're not looking at Silicon Valley, that needs mathematicians. They don't know.

It may appear that my position on community forces and community beliefs about mathematics holds African-Americans completely responsible for problematic outcomes in their mathematics achievement and persistence. It may also appear that my position implies that school-based issues of curriculum and pedagogy, teacher attitude, tracking, and unequal access to resources are not important factors in mathematics achievement and persistence among African-Americans. This is certainly not the case. In fact, my discussion of teachers in chapter 3 shows that I also advocate studying the backgrounds of teachers and accounting for the experiences that influence their interactions with and beliefs about African-American students, their parents, and their communities. In addition, my contentions about the effects of changes in the mathematics curriculum at Hillside highlight my concerns about how such changes, made in the name of reform, influence students' mathematics socializations, identities, and dispositions. Throughout my study, I was also aware of long-term district-level problems in Oakland that have continued to affect African-American students negatively and that continue to draw criticism from parents, community member, and advocates. I also attribute many of the problems that I observed at Hillside to these ongoing problems in the district.

My position on community forces is best characterized by the fact that I believe African-American parents and community members— teachers, curriculum, and resources aside—are the primary stakeholders in African-American students' success. Just as they have always been, these are the individuals who must continue to be the most forceful advocates for their children and who must monitor and demand accountability from and form partnerships with teachers and school officials. What happens in schools and mathematics classrooms among African-American children and their teachers should not be a mystery or intimidating to parents. Fears about mathematics, lingering feelings about their own experiences, and unintended messages about the importance of mathematics must be overcome if students are to have their best chance for success.

NO ONE SAID THERE WOULD BE DAYS LIKE THIS: MATHEMATICS SOCIALIZATION AMONG AFRICAN-AMERICAN STUDENTS AT HILLSIDE JUNIOR HIGH

In chapter 3, I set out to answer two questions: What was the nature of school-level forces at Hillside Junior High? How did interaction of these forces with larger community-level forces affect mathematics socialization among African-American students?

One important finding concerned the in-class negotiation of mathematical and social norms. This negotiation is what characterized days like those summarized in chapter 3 and reflected the fact that teachers and students brought their own distinct beliefs about mathematics and education into their classrooms. As we saw, these beliefs were not always compatible.

Brief biographical sketches showed that teachers, in their roles as agents of mathematics socialization, expressed beliefs and engaged in practices that were fueled by a host of factors including aspects of their own life histories; their expectations and goals for their students; their attempts to implement curricular change; demands placed on them by local, state, and national standards; and their attempts to reconcile what appeared to be competing demands between student-centered goals and content-related goals.

Much like successful teachers of African-American students portrayed elsewhere (e.g., Ladson-Billings, 1993, 1995) the mathematics teachers at Hillside could not be characterized as teachers who discriminated against African-American students or who treated them unfairly by tracking them out of mathematics. I found Mrs. Allgood, Mr. Olander, and Mr. Brown to be very firm and demanding but also very caring and committed to insuring that their students gain access to mathematics—an academic goal that was consistent with their collective concern for the betterment of the African-American community. Yet, in expressing the difficulties associated with achieving their goals, the teachers were honest and forthright in expressing their disappointment with the effort and attitude of many of their students and with the lack of support they received from parents.

Despite their tendency to be critical, math teachers at Hillside also acknowledged positive attributes of students and parents and maintained their efforts to get students to buy into the idea that mathematics was an important and necessary part of their lives. They did so by coming early and staying late to give students extra help, making themselves available at lunch time, or meeting as a group to discuss strategies to accomplish their goals.

On the other hand, my observations of students showed that they were not passive in their mathematics socializations. A disproportionate number of the students at Hillside displayed negative agency and appeared to be pulled toward low achievement and low motivation by a host of norms, beliefs, and behaviors that were common in their peer groups and that undermined the teacher-initiated efforts to help them.

In addition, day-to-day life in Mrs. Allgood's seventh grade classrooms often reflected a strong resistance to the curricular changes brought on by the mathematical and social demands of Algebra Project. Although this curriculum did stress many of the practices found in the NCTM *Standards,* many of the students questioned whether what they were doing was, in fact, "real" mathematics. These findings should be especially useful to curriculum developers. A curriculum that acts as a major context for students' mathematics socializations may embody many of the practices that we as educators would like students to embrace, but these curricula may also represent dramatic departures from the ways that students have grown accustomed to doing mathematics. Difficulties in adjustment by students may, in turn, adversely affect their beliefs about mathematics and their mathematics identities. This is a particularly relevant concern for African-American students, because of the many negative messages these students already receive about their abilities and opportunities to participate in mathematics. Curricular change should not be a process that contributes to these negative messages.

In my view, much of the disruptive behavior and lack of engagement demonstrated by some of the students at Hillside was correctly explained by Mr. Olander in chapter 3. He accurately pointed out that many students acted up in class because they wanted to draw attention to the fact that they were having difficulty adjusting to the demands being placed on them by the new practices stressed in their classrooms. As an observer and participant, I know that when students received the attention and assurance they apparently wanted, they often proceeded with their work and demonstrated the levels of understanding that were expected of them. When left on their own to struggle through some of the new practices, some students' frustration levels grew and they were more inclined to adopt an "I don't care" or "This isn't math" or "This is boring" attitude.

The negotiation process that was exemplified by students' resistance and the teachers' attempts to lessen this resistance was also exacerbated by the effects of certain community-level forces, including limited parental support. According to the teachers, and some of the students as well, this apparent lack of support may have sent students a message that some parents did not care about their children's performance and that mathematics was not important. This message, in turn, led many students to adopt attitudes and engage in behaviors that indicated that they did not care either.

The mix of contradictory messages students received from teachers, peers, and parents about the importance of mathematics knowledge was certainly a major factor in their achievement and classroom behaviors. Students were caught in the middle of the competing forces. They were also at stages in their adolescent and academic development where they were required to make difficult decisions about was and what was not important.

The literature on mathematics learning, achievement, and persistence among African-American students would lead us to believe that exposure to these external forces makes failure among these students inevitable. Although community and school forces did make it difficult for many students to totally invest in mathematics learning, the narratives from successful students showed that these forces do not always preclude mathematics success. In particular, the narratives presented in chapter 4 showed that students with strong personal, academic, and mathematics identities were able to effectively negotiate these forces and place a high priority on mathematics.

EXPLAINING ACADEMIC AND MATHEMATICS SUCCESS AMONG AFRICAN-AMERICAN STUDENTS: THE ROLE OF STUDENT AGENCY

As I indicated earlier, I believe that students at Hillside were, in many ways, caught between community forces and school forces. As they moved among community, classroom, and peer group contexts, they received various messages about mathematics. They also developed various beliefs about their mathematics abilities and about the instrumental importance of mathematics. This dynamic process of moving among these contexts and their construction of meanings for mathematics is what I believe constitutes a major, and understudied, part of African-American students' mathematics socializations.

The narratives in chapter 4 revealed that Black students are capable of displaying strong and positive individual agency in the face of these forces. Of course, there were also several other considerations that I took into account when I wanted to identify the forces responsible for students' success: Did they come from homes and communities that stressed the value and importance of education? Did they have role models and other important figures in their lives whom they wanted to emulate?

As it turns out, all of these considerations regarding why these students wanted to be successful were important—but in different ways for different students. This is important to note because it highlights the diversity that existed among the students and also helps explain why students who face similar circumstances can draw on different sources of motivation to help them achieve success. The students profiled in chapter 4 defied many of the characterizations of African-American students that are often found in the literature. Whatever objective circumstances characterized their home or school lives, these students did not let these circumstances determine their fates or define who they were or what they were capable of doing.

For example, it would be too simple to argue that students succeeded because they all received strong parental support. Some of the students, like Carl and Lisa, did mention that they received strong support and encouragement from their parents. But other students, like Melody, indicated that their parents asked very little and did not monitor their progress. Finally, other students, like Paulette, were not living with their parents at all and received their support from other family members—an indication that successful students were willing to draw motivation from whatever sources they deemed appropriate.

What I also found surprising was that, despite their differing backgrounds, different motivations, and the different sources of their support, there was also an important element of uniformity among the students. Nearly all of them emphasized the fact that they were motivated by an inner drive and self-determination to succeed:

Lisa: My parents encourage me. . . . I would say my whole family. . . . They just encourage me all the way. . . . [But] basically, it's just me. Me wanting to be somebody. I know if I want to become whatever I want to become, you have to have school. So I just stay on track. Think about school.

Paulette: I think it has a lot to do with the person that I am. Where I want to get to in life. I know what's ahead. . . . Second, my goals. What I expect in life and what I want. It's a need for me to be successful. That's what I want to do. My ambition is to help people. When I go downtown and the people I see in poverty. I don't feel we should live like that. So, if I'm successful then I know I can help somebody else be successful.

Annette: I know where I'm going. I know I'm going to go to college. I know that college is getting more expensive so I have to be the best or close to the best. . . . That's the way I am. It's not like my parents are pressuring me or my friends are pressuring me. It's just the way I feel. I think I'm kind of unique.

Melody: I would give part of the credit to me taking responsibility. . . . Me wanting the grades. . . . I feel that I have to do it on my own anyway. . . . [My mom] helps me get into programs and then I'll do it for myself from then on.

                        . . . .

DM: So do you feel shy about asking for help?

Carl: I'll ask for help but I feel that I should learn it on my own. If I know that I know something and I'm asking for help, I feel that's the wrong thing for me to do.

Another important finding was the degree to which these students strove toward success by engaging in what might be called self-definition by opposition to those elements of their surroundings that they perceived as negative. For example, all of the students were able to identify forces within their school context that they characterized as negative. First among these forces were the predominant attitudinal and behavioral norms of their peers. A majority of the successful students spoke about these peer group influences in ways that indicated they were motivated to be unlike their less successful peers:

DM: Do you think other kids think like you?

Lisa: No. Because most people don't care about school. Like some people cut [classes]. I don't see a point to cut. I don't see a point at all.

....

DM: You mentioned a couple of times that you feel it falls on you, that it's your responsibility [to do well]. You also mentioned that sometimes other kids do different things. Do you let that stuff get in your way?

Melody: No. Not really. . . . A lot of the students, how they act, I wouldn't want to act like that. That's my motto—to not act how they act.

Students also appeared to have a keen awareness of the forces that extended beyond their school context, among them the social conditions that had affected people in their communities, including their own families. An excerpt from my interview with Melody proved to be an excellent example of the ability of students to recognize and respond effectively to these forces. In that excerpt, reproduced here, Melody referred to conditions in her own home that motivated her to do well:

DM: Is that one of the biggest reasons for you [to think math is important], to get a good job?

Melody: Uh huh. I don't want to struggle for nothing if I don't have to. I want to live a decent life. I don't want to be rich or anything. I want to be able to provide for my kids if I have to. I don't want us to have to struggle month by month.

DM: Do you see other people that have to go through that struggle? Where are you getting that image from?

Melody: From myself, my own family. I [say to myself] I do not want to be like this when I grow up. My mom had a

good job. . . . She decided to quit. She had a good job
and we were doing good. I was [thinking], "Why did
she do that?"

....

DM: Does your mom know about the way you think?

Melody: Yes. I tell her, I'm not going to be like you. . . . She's a
good mom. She provides for us in every way she can
. . . . But I don't want to have to struggle.

Perhaps most troubling in my analysis of student success was the
fact that successful students had to face and deal effectively with
differential treatment from their peers. This treatment ranged from
minor taunts such as being called "nerd" to more serious accusations
of trying to "act White." As an indication of their personal strength
and resolve to succeed, most of the students did not let these comments
deter them from striving toward their goals. Indeed, most used these
outside challenges to their personal and cultural identities as
motivation to do even better.

My purpose in highlighting these particular aspects of African-
American students' success is to point out that, although community
and school forces do have the potential to affect their mathematics
socializations and identities, these forces are not deterministic. Students
are capable of recognizing and responding to these forces in ways that
help them resist the negative forces and to take advantage of the
positive forces that they encounter.

Contributions and Implications

I conclude this chapter by discussing the contributions and
implications of this research for mathematics educators, African-
American parents and community members, African-American
students, and teachers of African-American students. I believe this
book makes several contributions to our understanding of mathematics
learning, achievement, and persistence among African-Americans.

Methods

Because of the long-standing nature of problematic outcomes in
mathematics achievement and persistence among African-Americans,
lack of compelling explanations for these problems, and lack of

knowledge of mathematics success among African-American students, there is a clear need for more systematic approaches to investigating mathematics achievement and persistence. These approaches should complement rather than duplicate what we already know about testing, tracking, and course-taking patterns and should incorporate aspects of ethnographic and participant observation methods to obtain first-hand accounts of the mathematical experiences of African-American parents and students. Most important, these approaches should attempt to examine community forces, school forces, and intrapersonal agency forces within the same analysis. Given that prior studies of mathematics learning among African-Americans have not addressed issues of socialization and identity in detail or at sufficient levels of complexity, a major goal of this book is to utilize an appropriate collection of methods that would allow me to investigate the meanings for mathematics learning and knowledge that were developed by the participants as well as the experiences that gave rise to these meanings.

Utilizing ethnographic and participant observations and interviews in classroom and community contexts, student surveys, and fine-grained analyses of participant narratives, this goal was accomplished to the degree that I was able to offer rich descriptions of mathematics socialization that explained how and why African-American parents, community members, students, and their teachers defined mathematics knowledge in the ways that they did.

Mathematics Socialization and Identity

Given the analyses in chapters 2, 3, and 4, it is my firm belief that detailed analyses of mathematics socialization and identity—and the multiple contexts that affect them—offer the best hope for understanding long-standing achievement and persistence issues. As these experiences, and the beliefs that grow out of them, continue to be unpacked and analyzed, it will become even more apparent that conventional explanations, which ignore mathematics socialization and identity, do not adequately explain these issues. Unless we begin to uncover and understand the meanings that mathematics knowledge assumes for students, parents, and their communities and how these meanings are internalized to produce productive or unproductive agency, attempts to alter achievement and persistence results by manipulating variables only inside the school will have little effect in reversing negative trends.

Of course mathematics socialization and identity are developmental processes, and my study represented only a snapshot of these processes for the participants in my study. Therefore, my research does not imply or predict that things will remain the same with the students and teachers at Hillside or with the parents and community members who participated in my study. Students who were not doing well in the course of my study may have reversed their achievement. Students who were doing well may have fallen prey to negative influences. I also know that that Mr. Olander and Mr. Brown both left Hillside for better opportunities to teach elsewhere and that the Algebra Project curriculum is no longer in use at Hillside. Perhaps some of the parents and community members whom I interviewed have gone on to develop consistently positive mathematical beliefs and mathematics identities, thereby contributing to the kinds of community beliefs about mathematics that I believe students need to help them succeed.

Focus on Student Success and Agency

This research also contributes new knowledge about mathematics success among African-American students and demonstrates how both success and failure can be found within the same sets of social and school conditions previously thought of as only producing failure. The analyses in chapter 4 showed that successful students can respond effectively to these conditions by adopting strong personal, academic, and mathematics identities and by engaging in self-definition in the direction of success by resisting and opposing what they perceive as negative or as obstacles that stand in the way of their goals.

Implications for African-American Parents and Community Members

In many ways, African-American parents and community members are the conduits for change in helping reverse problematic achievement and persistence trends among African-American students. Although they may have experienced negative mathematics socializations themselves and have been adversely affected by larger sociohistorical and socioeconomic forces, it is imperative that parents struggle to fight off the effects of these experiences. They must stress more forcefully the importance of mathematics knowledge for their children. These messages about its importance should not represent simple rhetorical support and imply that mathematics is only valuable as an important school subject. They should be backed up by appropriate action and should also imply that mathematics is important for instrumental reasons. It is my strong belief that unless African-American communities begin to think of mathematical literacy in civil rights terms—as has been advocated by Robert Moses—or to develop cultural frames of reference that elevate the pursuit of mathematics knowledge as an ideal way of behaving, students will be left on their own to wade through an endless stream of mixed and contradictory messages about its importance.

Implications for African-American Students

The discussion in chapter 4 showed that mathematics success among African-American students is attainable. This success is not determined in any straightforward way by student ability, family background, or teacher attitude. What it also depends on is how students respond to the forces around them. It is important that African-American students begin to associate the learning of mathematics not with being a "nerd" or with attempts to "act White" but with attempts to succeed and take advantage of what life has to offer. Students must be helped to realize that mathematics knowledge is like a key. It can open many doors. It is true that these doors were previously closed to their parents and other members of their communities and that access to some of these doors is still limited. But if students choose not to invest in mathematics learning, based on the experiences of their parents and community members, then they not only lose access to the key that is represented by mathematics knowledge, but they lose access to the opportunities mathematics has to offer as well. Not possessing this knowledge places them on the periphery of a society that is now characterized by growing demand for those who will possess the mathematical and technical skills of the 21st century. Without such skills, African-American students will never have the opportunity to become legitimate participants and full citizens in this newly emerging society.

Implications for Teachers and
Mathematics Education Researchers

In my view, the implications of this research for mathematics educators are clear. If long-standing issues in achievement and persistence are to be understood more fully, they must be examined not simply in the context of testing, teacher attitude, curricular change, or the personal backgrounds of students. These issues must also be examined within their broader sociohistorical and socioeconomic contexts. In addition, there is also a need to reexamine our assumptions and prior perspectives on community and school forces. For example, the analyses in chapter 3 showed that in discussing curricular change, it was not enough to analyze how these changes affected teaching and learning in mathematics classrooms at Hillside. It was also imperative to understand and recognize that community forces made it difficult for such change to be successful.

Moreover, it will not be enough for teachers, school officials, and mathematics education researchers to simply acknowledge the role and importance of contextual forces. It will also become imperative that such knowledge be used as a guiding principle in our efforts to tackle tough issues associated with mathematics achievement and persistence and in carrying out research that purports to explain problematic outcomes.

Finally, teachers, school officials, and researchers must develop effective strategies for helping African-American communities, parents, and students stress the importance of mathematics beyond the school context and for supporting students who succeed in light of or in spite of the factors that we think should only contribute to their failure.

Concluding Remarks

Prior research on mathematics learning has made it very clear that African-American students do not persist or achieve to their potential in mathematics. However, despite our increased understandings of how students learn, how teachers teach, and improved methods of assessing teachers and students, mathematics educators have yet to offer compelling accounts as to why these trends have persisted. This book documented small portions of mathematics socialization, identity, and success among African-Americans and addressed several questions related to how these socializations, identities, and successes were influenced by sociohistorical, community, school, and intrapersonal forces. It is my hope that the theoretical framework, methods of analysis, and results in my study can be useful in furthering our efforts to improve and more completely understand mathematics success and failure among African-Americans.

References

Anderson, J. (1988). *The education of Blacks in the south, 1860–1935.* Chapel Hill: University of North Carolina Press.

Anick, C. M., Carpenter, T. P., & Smith, C. (1981). Minorities and mathematics: Results from the National Assessment of Educational Progress. *Mathematics Teacher, 74,* 560–566.

Atweh, B., Bleicher, R., & Cooper, T. (1995, April). *Social context in mathematics classrooms: Social critical and sociolinguistic perspectives.* Paper presented at the annual meeting of the American Educational Research Association, San Francisco.

Bandura, A. (1982). Self-efficacy mechanism in human agency. *American Psychologist, 37,* 122–147.

Bandura, A. (1986). *Social foundations of thought and action: A social cognitive theory.* Englewood Cliffs, NJ: Prentice-Hall.

Bandura, A. (1997). *Self-efficacy: The exercise of control.* New York: W. H. Freeman and Company.

Betz, N. E. (1991). *What stops women and minorities from choosing and completing majors in engineering and science?* Washington, DC: Federation of Behavioral, Psychological, and Cognitive Sciences.

Bishop, A. (1988). *Mathematical enculturation: A cultural perspective on mathematics education.* London: Kluwer Academic Press.

Bowles, S., & Gintis, H. (1976). *Schooling in capitalist America.* New York: Basic Books.

Brown, C. A., & Borko, H. (1992). Becoming a mathematics teacher. In D. Grouws (Ed.), *Handbook for research on mathematics teaching and learning* (pp. 209–239). New York: Macmillan.

California State Department of Education. (1992). *Mathematics framework for California public schools kindergarten through grade twelve.* Sacramento: California State Department of Education.

Carey, D., Fennema, E., Carpenter, T., & Franke, M. (1995). Equity in mathematics education. In W. Secada, E. Fennema, & L. Byrd Adajian (Eds.), *New directions for equity in mathematics education* (pp. 93–125). New York: Cambridge University Press.

Carr, M. (1996). *Motivation in mathematics.* Creskill, NJ: Hampton Press.

Clark, R. (1984). *Family life and school achievement: Why poor Black children succeed or fail.* Chicago: University of Chicago Press.

Clewell, B., Anderson, B., & Thorpe, M. (1992). *Breaking the barriers: Helping female and minority students succeed in mathematics and science.* San Francisco: Jossey-Bass.

Comer, J. (1980). *School power.* New York: Free Press.

Cross, Jr., W. E. (1991). *Shades of Black: Diversity in African-American identity.* Philadelphia: Temple University Press.

Delpit, L. (1988). The silenced dialogue: Power and pedagogy in educating other people's children. *Harvard Educational Review, 58*(3), 280–298.

Dossey, J. A., Mullis, I. V. S., Lindquist, M. M., & Chambers, D. L. (1988). *The mathematics report card.* Princeton, NJ: National Assessment of Educational Progress.

Eccles, J., Lord, S., & Midgeley, C. (1991). What are we doing to early adolescents? The impact of educational contexts on early adolescents. *American Journal of Education, 99,* 521–542.

Eisenhart, M. (1988). The ethnographic research tradition in mathematics education research. *Journal for Research in Mathematics Education, 19*(2), 99–114.

Fennema, E., & Loef Franke, M. (1992). Teachers' knowledge and its impact. In D. Grouws (Ed.), *Handbook for research on mathematics teaching and learning* (pp. 147–164). New York: Macmillan.

Fordham, S. (1988). Racelessness as a factor in Black students' school success: Pragmatic strategy or pyrrhic victory? *Harvard Educational Review, 58*(1), 54–84.

Fordham, S. (1993). Those loud Black girls: (Black) women, silence, and gender "passing" in the Academy. *Anthropology and Education Quarterly, 24,* 3–32.

Fordham, S. (1996). *Blacked out: Dilemmas of race, identity, and success at Capital High.* Chicago: University of Chicago Press.

Fordham, S., & Ogbu, J. U. (1986). Black students' school success: Coping with the burden of acting White. *Urban Review, 18*(3), 176–206.

Frankenstein, M. (1995). Equity in mathematics education: Class in the world outside of class. In W. Secada, E. Fennema, & L. Byrd Adajian (Eds.), *New directions for equity in mathematics education* (pp. 164–190). New York: Cambridge University Press.

Gay, J., & Cole, M. (1967). *The new mathematics and an old culture: A study of learning among the Kpelle of Liberia.* New York: Holt.

Gibson, M. A. (1987). The school performance of immigrant minorities: A comparative view. *Anthropology and Education Quarterly, 18*(4), 262–275.

Ginsburg, H. P., & Russell, R. L. (1981). Social class and racial influences on early mathematical thinking. *Monographs of the Society for Research in Child Development, 46,* (Serial No. 6).

Graham, S. (1994). Motivation in African-Americans. *Review of Educational Research, 64*(1), 55–117.

Hale-Benson, J. E. (1994). *Unbank the fire: Visions for the education of African-American children.* Baltimore: Johns Hopkins University Press.

Hart, L. E. (1989). *Describing the affective domain: Saying what we mean.* New York: Springer Verlag.

Hart, L., & Allexsaht-Snider, M. (1996). Sociocultural and motivational contexts of mathematics learning for diverse students. In M. Carr (Ed.), *Motivation in mathematics* (pp. 1–24). Creskill, NJ: Hampton Press.

Haynes, N., & Comer, J. (1990). Helping Black children succeed: The significance of some social factors. In K. Lomotey (Ed.), *Going to school: The African-American experience* (pp. 103–112). Albany: State University of New York Press.

Hems, J. E. (1990). *Black and White racial identity: Theory, research, and practice.* Westport, CT: Greenwood, 1990.

Herrnstein, R. J., & Murray, C. (1994). *The bell curve: Intelligence and class structure in American life.* New York: Free Press.

Johnson, M. L. (1984). Blacks in mathematics: A status report. *Journal for Research in Mathematics Education, 15,* 145–153.

Johnson, M. L. (1989). Minority differences in mathematics. In M. M. Lindquist (Ed.), *Results from the fourth mathematics assessment of the National Assessment of Education Progress* (pp. 135–148). Reston, VA: National Council of Teachers of Mathematics.

Jones, J. (1993). Psychosocial aspects of cultural influences on learning mathematics and science. In J. Greeno (Ed.),*The challenge in mathematics and science education: Psychology's response* (pp. 205–236). Washington, DC: American Psychological Association.

Jones, L. V., Burton, N. W., & Davenport, E. C. (1984). Monitoring the mathematics achievement of Black students. *Journal for Research in Mathematics Education, 15,* 154–164.

King, J. (1991). Dysconscious racism: Ideology, identity, and the miseducation of teachers. *Journal of Negro Education, 60*(2), 133–146.

Knoff, H. (1993). Applied psychological research on mathematics and science education. In J. Greeno (Ed.), *The challenge in mathematics and science education: Psychology's* response (pp. 277–286). Washington, DC: American Psychological Association.

Ladson-Billings, G. (1993, March). *Skills and other dilemmas revisited: Issues of equity and achievement in mathematics.* Paper presented at the research presession of the annual meeting of the National Council of Teachers of Mathematics, Seattle.

Ladson-Billings, G. (1994). *The dreamkeepers: Successful teachers of African-American children.* San Francisco: Jossey-Bass.

Ladson-Billings, G. (1995). Toward a theory of culturally relevant pedagogy. *American Educational Research Journal, 32*(3), 465–492.

Luster, L. (1992). *Schooling, survival, and struggle; Black women and the GED.* Unpublished doctoral dissertation, School of Education, Stanford University.

Matthews, W. (1984). Influences on the learning and participation of minorities in mathematics. *Journal for Research in Mathematics Education, 15*(2) 84–95.

Matthews, W., Carpenter, T. P., Lindquist, M. M., & Silver, E. A. (1984). The third national assessment: Minorities and mathematics. *Journal for Research in Mathematics Education, 15,* 165–171.

McLeod, D. (1992). Research on affect in mathematics learning; A reconceptualization. In D. Grouws (Ed.), *Handbook for research on mathematics teaching and learning* (pp. 575–596). New York: Macmillan.

Meece, J. (1991). The classroom context and students' motivational goals. In M. L. Maeher & P. R. Pintrich (Eds.), *Advances in motivation and achievement* (Vol. 7, pp. 261–286). Greenwich, CT: JAI Press.

Mickelson, R. (1990). The attitude-achievement paradox among Black adolescents. *Sociology of Education, 63,* 44–61.

Monthly Labor Review (November, 1997). *Occupational employment projections to 2006* (pp. 58–83). Washington, DC: Bureau of Labor Statistics.

Moses, R. P. (1994). Remarks on the struggle for citizenship and math/science literacy. *Journal of Mathematical Behavior, 13,* 107–111.

Moses, R. P., Kamii, M., Swap, S., & Howard, J. (1989). The Algebra Project: Organizing in the spirit of Ella. *Harvard Educational Review, 59*(4), 423–443.

National Center for Educational Statistics (1997). *The condition of education, 1997.* Washington, DC: U.S. Department of Education.

National Council of Teachers of Mathematics. (1989). *Curriculum and evaluation standards for school mathematics.* Reston, VA: Author.

Nieto, S. (1996). *Affirming diversity: The sociopolitical context of multicultural education.* New York: Longman.

Noddings, N. (1992). Professionalism and mathematics teaching. In D. Grouws (Ed.), *Handbook for research on mathematics teaching and learning* (pp. 197–208). New York: Macmillan.

Nunes, T. (1992). Ethnomathematics and everyday cognition. In D. Grouws (Ed.), *Handbook of research on mathematics teaching and learning* (pp. 557–574). New York: Macmillan.

Oakes, J. (1985). *Keeping track: How schools structure inequality.* New Haven, CT: Yale University Press.

Oakes, J. (1990a) *Multiplying inequalities: The effects of race, social class, and tracking on opportunities to learn mathematics and science.* Santa Monica, CA: Rand Corporation.

Oakes, J. (1990b). Opportunities, achievement and choice: Women and minority students in science and mathematics. In C. B. Cazden (Ed.), *Review of research in education, 16* (pp. 153–222). Washington, DC: American Educational Research Association.

Oakland California Unified School District. (1993). *Mathematics core curriculum, grades K–8*. Oakland: Author.

O'Connor, C. (1997). Dispositions toward (collective) struggle and educational resilience in the inner city: A case analysis of six African-American high school students. *American Educational Research Journal, 34*(4), 593–629.

Ogbu, J. U. (1974). *The next generation: An ethnography of schooling in an urban neighborhood.* New York: Academic Press.

Ogbu, J. U. (1987a). Opportunity structure, cultural boundaries, and literacy. In J. A. Langer (Ed.), *Language, literacy, and culture: Issues of society and schooling* (pp. 149–177). Norwood, NJ: Ablex.

Ogbu, J. U. (1987b). Variability in minority school performance: A problem in search of an explanation. *Anthropology and Education Quarterly, 18*(4), 312–334.

Ogbu, J. U. (1988). Diversity and equity in public education: Community forces and minority school adjustment and performance. In R. Haskins & D. McRae (Eds.), *Policies for America's public schools: Teachers, equity, and indicators* (pp. 127–170). Norwood, NJ: Ablex.

Ogbu, J. U. (1989a). *Cultural models and educational strategies of non-dominant peoples.* 1989 Catherine Molony Memorial Lecture.

Ogbu, J. U. (1989b). The individual in collective adaptation: A framework for focusing on academic under performance and dropping out among involuntary minorities. In L. Weis, E. Farrar, & H. Petrie (Eds.), *Dropouts from school: Issues, dilemmas, and solutions* (pp. 198–204). Buffalo: State University of New York Press.

Ogbu, J. U. (1990). Cultural model, identity, and literacy. In J. W. Stigler, R. A. Shweder, & G. Herdt (Eds.), *Cultural Psychology,* 520–541. Cambridge: Cambridge University Press.

Ogbu, J. U. (1992a). Adaptation to minority status and impact on school success. *Theory into practice, 31*(4), 287–295.

Ogbu, J. U. (1992b). Understanding cultural diversity and learning. *Educational Researcher, 21*(8), 5–14.

Ogbu, J. U. (1993). Differences in cultural frame of reference. *International Journal of Behavioral Development, 16*(3), 483–506.

Orr, E. (1987). *Twice as less: Black English and the performance of Black students in mathematics and science.* New York: Norton.

Patterson, J. (1991). Minorities gain but gaps remain. *Peabody Journal of Education, 66*(2), 72–94.

Patterson, O. (1997). *The ordeal of integration.* Washington, DC: CIVITAS.

Post, P., Stewart, M. A., & Smith, P. L. (1991). Self-efficacy, interest, and consideration of math/science and non math/science occupations among college freshman. *Journal of Vocational Behavior, 38,* 179–186.

Resnick, L. B. (1989). Treating mathematics as an ill-structured discipline. In R. I. Charles & E. A. Silver (Eds.), *The teaching and assessing of mathematical problem solving* (pp. 32–60). Hillsdale, NJ: Lawrence Erlbaum Associates.

Reyes, L. H. (1984). Affective variables and mathematics education. *Elementary School Journal, 84,* 558–581.

Reyes, L. H., & Stanic, G. (1988). Race, sex, socioeconomic status, and mathematics. *Journal for Research in Mathematics Education, 19,* 26–43.

Samimy, K., Liu, L., & Matsuta, K. (1994). Gambare, Amae, and Giri: A cultural explanation for Japanese children's success in mathematics. *Journal of Mathematical Behavior, 13,* 261–271.

Saxe, G. (1992). *Culture and cognitive development: Studies in mathematical understanding.* Hillsdale, NJ: Lawrence Erlbaum Associates.

Schoenfeld, A. (1992). Learning to think mathematically: Problem solving, metacognition and sense making in mathematics. In D. Grouws (Ed.), *Handbook for research on mathematics teaching and learning* (pp. 334–370). New York: Macmillan.

Schultz, K. (1996). Between work and work: The literacies of urban adolescent females. *Anthropology and Education Quarterly, 27*(3), 517–544.

Secada, W. (1992). Race, ethnicity, social class, language and achievement in mathematics. In D. Grouws (Ed.), *Handbook of research on mathematics teaching and learning* (pp. 146–164). New York: Macmillan.

Secada, W. (1995). Social and critical dimensions for equity in mathematics education. In W. Secada, E. Fennema, & L. Adajian (Eds.), *New directions for equity in mathematics education* (pp. 246–164). New York: Cambridge University Press.

Secada, W., Ogbu, J. U., Peterson, P., Stiff, L. M., & Tonemah, S. (1994). *At the intersection of school mathematics and student diversity: A challenge to research and reform.* Washington, DC: Mathematical Sciences Education Board and National Academy of Education.

Shulman, J., & Mesa-Bains, A. (1990). *Teaching diverse students: Cases and commentaries.* San Francisco: Far West Laboratory for Educational Research and Development.

Silva, C. M., & Moses, R. P. (1990). The algebra project: Making middle school mathematics count. *Journal of Negro Education, 59*(3), 375–391.

Silver, E. A., Smith, M., & Scott Nelson, B. (1995). The QUASAR Project: Equity concerns meet mathematics reform in the middle school. In W. Secada, E. Fennema, & L. Byrd Adajian (Eds.), *New directions for equity in mathematics education* (pp. 9–56). New York: Cambridge University Press.

Smith, M. (1995). Color blindness and basket weaving are not the answer: Confronting the dilemmas of race, culture, and language diversity. *American Educational Research Association, 32*(3), 493–523.

Stanic, G. (1991). Social inequality, cultural discontinuity, and equity in school mathematics. *Peabody Journal of Education, 66*(2), 57–71.

Stanic, G., & Hart, L. (1995). Attitudes, persistence, and mathematics achievement: Qualifying race and sex differences. In W. Secada, E. Fennema, & L. Byrd Adajian (Eds.), *New directions for equity in mathematics education* (pp. 258–278). New York: Cambridge University Press.

Stevenson, H., & Stigler, J. (1992). *The learning gap.* New York: Touchstone.

Stiff, L. V. (1990). African-American students and the promise of the curriculum and evaluation standards. In T. J. Cooney & C. R. Hirsch (Eds.), *Teaching and learning mathematics in the 1990's.* Reston, VA: NCTM.

Tate, W. F. (1994). Race, retrenchment, and the reform of school mathematics. *Phi delta kappan, 75*(6), 477–485.

Tate, W. F. (1995). Economics, equity, and the national mathematics assessment: Are we creating a national toll road? In W. Secada, E. Fennema, & L. Byrd Adajian (Eds.), *New directions for equity in mathematics in mathematics education* (pp. 191–208). New York: Cambridge University Press.

Tatum, B. D. (1997). *Why are all the Black kids sitting together in the cafeteria?* New York: Basic Books.

Thompson, A. (1985). Teacher's conceptions of mathematics and the teaching of problem solving. In E. A. Silver (Ed.), *Teaching and learning mathematical problem solving: Multiple research perspectives* (pp. 281–294). Hillsdale, NJ: Lawrence Erlbaum Associates.

Thompson, A. (1992). Teachers' beliefs and conceptions: A synthesis of the research. In D. Grouws (Ed.), *Handbook of research on mathematics teaching and learning* (pp. 127–146). New York: Macmillan.

Treisman, P. U. (1985). *A study of the mathematics performance of Black students at the University of California, Berkeley.* Unpublished doctoral dissertation, Berkeley, CA.

Trueba, H. (1988). Culturally based explanations of minority students' academic achievement. *Anthropology and Education Quarterly, 19,* 270–287.

Tsang, S. (1988). The mathematics achievement characteristics of Asian American students. In R. R. Cocking & J. P. Mestre (Eds.), *Linguistic and cultural influences on learning mathematics* (pp. 123–136). Hillsdale, NJ: Lawrence Erlbaum Associates.

Weis, L., & Fine, M. (1996). Narrating the 1980s and 1990s: Voices of poor and working-class White and African-American men. *Anthropology and Education Quarterly, 27*(4), 493–516.

Welch, O., & Hodges, C. (1997). *Standing on the outside on the inside: Black adolescents and the construction of academic identity.* Albany: State University of New York Press.

Willis, P. (1977). *Learning to labor.* New York: Columbia University Press.

Wilson, W. J. (1987). *The truly disadvantaged: The inner city, the underclass, and public policy.* Chicago: University of Chicago Press.

Wilson, W. J. (1996). *When work disappears.* New York: Vintage Books.

Winfield, L. (1986). Teacher beliefs toward at-risk students in inner-city urban schools. *Urban Review, 18*(4), 253–267.

Woodson. C. G. (1990). *The mis-education of the Negro.* Nashville: Winston-Derek Publishers, Inc. (Original work published 1933)

Author Index

Subject Index